# Architectural Lighting: Designing with Light and Space

The **Architecture Briefs** series takes on a variety of single topics of interest to architecture students and young professionals. Field-specific information and digital techniques are presented in a user-friendly manner along with basic principles of design and construction. The series familiarizes readers with the concepts and technical terms necessary to successfully translate ideas into built form.

Also in this series:
*Architectural Photography: The Digital Way*, Gerry Kopelow
*Architects Draw*, Sue Ferguson Gussow
*Digital Fabrications*, Lisa Iwamoto
*Building Envelopes*, Jenny Lovell
*Ethics for Architects*, Thomas Fisher

**Architecture Briefs**
The Foundations of Architecture

# Architectural Lighting: Designing with Light and Space

**Hervé Descottes**
with Cecilia E. Ramos

Princeton Architectural Press
New York

Published by
Princeton Architectural Press
37 East Seventh Street
New York, New York 10003

For a free catalog of books, call 1.800.722.6657.
Visit our website at www.papress.com.

Editor: Becca Casbon
Designer: Jan Haux

Special thanks to: Bree Anne Apperley, Sara Bader, Nicola Bednarek
Brower, Janet Behning, Carina Cha, Tom Cho, Penny (Yuen Pik)
Chu, Russell Fernandez, Pete Fitzpatrick, Jan Haux, Linda Lee, John
Myers, Katharine Myers, Dan Simon, Andrew Stepanian, Jennifer
Thompson, Paul Wagner, Joseph Weston, and Deb Wood of Princeton
Architectural Press —Kevin C. Lippert, publisher

Library of Congress Cataloging-in-Publication Data
Descottes, Hervé.
Architectural lighting : designing with light and space / Hervé
Descottes, coauthor Cecilia E. Ramos. -- 1st ed.
   p. cm. -- (Architecture briefs)
Includes bibliographical references and index.
ISBN 978-1-56898-938-9 (alk. paper)
1. Light in architecture. 2. Lighting. I. Ramos, Cecilia E. II. Title.
NA2794.D47 2011
729'.28--dc22
                               2010027086

# Contents

# Acknowledgments

I am grateful to the many who helped me bring this book to fruition, and without whose support I would be at a loss. First I would like to thank Cecilia E. Ramos for her research and writing contributions to *Architectural Lighting*, and for her dedication and determination in making this project happen. Second I would like to extend my thanks to Princeton Architectural Press for this wonderful opportunity, specifically to Clare Jacobson, who supported the project from its conceptual beginnings, and to Becca Casbon, who steered it through to publication. I am grateful to my three friends and colleagues who graciously contributed to the contents of this book: to Steven Holl, for his inspiration, poetry, friendship, and for the many wonderful professional moments we have shared; to Sylvain Dubuisson, for his continuous inspiration, insight, and friendship; and to James Corner, for the opportunity to work on so many beautiful projects together. The illustrations for this book were completed by Anna Muzlimova, and I thank her for her beautiful work and for the many years of collaboration with her. Also, the book would not look quite the same without the superb images of the many photographers who generously contributed their work to this project. A big thank you goes to B. Alex Miller and Socorro Sperati for the constructive conversations we have shared, and for their feedback and general review of this book. A special thanks to Miina Matsuoka for our partnership, our closeness, and for her ongoing support. And a final thank you to the L'Observatoire International team of the past, present, and future, with whom I have had the pleasure to share so many important moments throughout many wonderful projects.

—Hervé Descottes

# Introduction

We find beauty not in the thing itself, but in the patterns of shadows, the light and the darkness, that one thing against another creates.

—Jun'ichirō Tanizaki

Our visual understanding of this world is defined through both material and light, two seemingly opposite phenomena inextricably linked to one another. Light is revealed to the human eye through interactions with material, while material visually exists only in the presence of light. This interdependence between material and light, form and intangible atmospheres, defines the visual environments we inhabit.

While light is by definition energy, its effects transgress the realm of the scientific, moving into that of the experiential. Light renders our world in an endless array of visual permutations, revealing colors, textures, distances, or the passing of time. These and other qualities of light can affect emotions and trigger memories, giving rise to specificity of place. What we often recall of a space is its feeling or sense of "atmosphere," not its formal details. On a practical level, light ensures visibility, and through the definition of visual limits it can establish spatial hierarchies and sequences, or spaces of movement and pause. As architectural lighting designers, our role is to utilize light as a medium through which architectural intentions can be heightened and experiential spaces transformed.

Architectural lighting design is a discipline cultivated from a myriad of fields: architecture, art, and engineering are but a few sources of knowledge from which we draw. This pluralistic model is both the foundation and the point of departure for the emergence of lighting design as its own specialty.

Similarly, the history of architectural lighting does not unfold in a singular trajectory. Instead, independent narratives can be woven together to tell its story, as humans sought to harness light in pursuit of spirituality, in the name of social organization, or for practical or aesthetic purposes in the built environment. The evolution of architectural lighting design is invariably linked to the emergence of new architectural forms, technologies, and the innovative visions of many. We can look to the oculus of the Pantheon, the spinning chandeliers of a Byzantine church, or the emergence of the nineteenth-century gas street lamp as benchmarks in our complex history. Only in the twentieth century, however, did the independent discipline of lighting design coalesce, replete with its own professional constituency.

In the twenty-first century, architectural lighting design continues to practice in concert with many other fields. While lighting design's primary purpose is to respond to the needs of a space, to do so successfully requires the active collaboration of all parties involved, including but not limited to the client, architect, interior designer, landscape architect, urban planner, and engineers. Moreover, an architectural lighting designer's work is not limited to the realm of aesthetics, but also responds to functional, technical, spatial, and experiential necessities of a project. Lighting design necessitates a deep, meditative exchange of knowledge, and therefore it must be understood not as an interdisciplinary field but as a transdisciplinary one that traverses the boundaries of conventional thought.

With regard to this history and practical trajectory, it is necessary to underscore two vital issues specific to the methodologies of this book. First, while this book will certainly draw upon overlaps in a variety of professions, we will focus primarily on the application of lighting in the built environment and the ways in which light can create and alter our perception of these spaces. Second, it must be noted that this publication provides a particular approach to the profession that has been garnered through Hervé Descottes's personal experiences in

the field and through his relationships with architects, collaborators, and his firm, L'Observatoire International, so the methods of lighting design examined here are not to be considered exhaustive. We have not written an encyclopedic book on the science and technologies of lighting, nor do we aim to tell a history of architectural lighting design—these stories can be found elsewhere. Instead, we wish to provide the reader with new insight on the experiential potential of architectural lighting design in light of Descottes's reflections and experiences.

The issues central to this publication are explored both theoretically and analytically; this duality provides the conceptual framework to our book, mirroring the relative nature of light and material. *Architectural Lighting* is thus structured as two major sections. The first explores what we call the six visual principles of light—a set of design parameters essential to the philosophies of Descottes—and the ways in which these principles can be controlled and adapted to optimally render definitive built environments. The second section explains and illustrates six built projects, giving specificity to the previous theoretical exploration while providing our readers with concrete examples of the way in which these principles are applied to architecture. Following this main content is a collection of short essays on the power of lighting and its role in defining architectural, spatial, and social compositions, written by a prominent architect, a landscape architect, and an interior designer who have all worked closely with L'Observatoire International to define the environments of their fields. In conclusion, a brief series of appendices summarize what we consider to be essential technical and practical knowledge relevant to this discipline. Together, we hope that these theoretical and analytical explorations will provide new insight into the work of architectural lighting designers today.

# Six Visual Principles of Light

The six visual principles of light presented in this section are a set of design parameters central to L'Observatoire International's approach to lighting design. This method for qualifying the role of light in a space was first introduced to Hervé Descottes by lighting designer, sculptor, and philosopher Philippe de Bozzi in 1989, and has since been adapted and expanded by Descottes into a guide that steers theoretical and practical aspects of the firm's work. Like an aviation checklist, the six visual principles provide a verifiable list of factors to be considered when lighting architectural spaces. However, while each principle is certainly of individual importance, ultimately they must operate in tandem—both with one another as well as with the surrounding architecture—to create the desired spatial experience. In this sense, the individual principles alone are but fractional pieces of a greater puzzle that, when joined together, achieve a single vision through relative interaction.

The six principles—illuminance, luminance, color and temperature, height, density, and direction and distribution—are empirical by nature, but their quantifiable measures embody only a portion of their working potential. More importantly, each principle addresses a set of visual factors that are not easily measured. By defining the six principles, we aim to establish a common vocabulary through which the visual and experiential aspects of lighting design can also be properly addressed. We hope that the explanation and discussion of these principles will facilitate the dialogue regarding the visual relationship between light and space.

# Illuminance

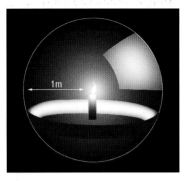

**1.1** A lux is defined as the sphere of illumination cast by a one-candela point source on a surface one meter away.

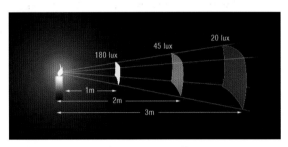

**1.2** Illumination as a function of distance: Illumination decreases as the distance between the light source and the illuminated area increases.

Illuminance quite simply describes the quantity of light emitted by a light source that lands on a given surface area, measured in footcandles or, in the metric system, lux. 1.1 and 1.2 In the built environment, illuminance is the feature that brings shape and clarity to a nuanced spatial composition. It is capable of controlling the intensity of visual extremes, crescendos of light and dark that can both reveal and hide layers of a complex space. This principle is of great practical and phenomenological importance in architectural lighting design, as it allows us to navigate our way through, or perform tasks within, a space. Illuminance, moreover, plays a critical role in our emotional response to a space: our intrinsic fear of the dark or gravitation toward light has influenced the ways in which our society places faith in light as a means to establish safety and provide emotional reassurance. Finally, one must not forget that the term "illuminance" describes a quantity of light or energy that, when administered at the appropriate levels, ensures the sustenance of life, but when pushed to extremes, can cause physical damage to its recipient. For these reasons, the careful control of illuminance is essential to provide visibility, safety, and emotional satisfaction.

# Visibility

Light is the primary means through which we engage with our surroundings. Light and vision reveal an incomprehensible scale and limitless depth of our perceived worlds that no other sense can render. 1.3 Of the five senses, if we were to depend solely on touch or taste, the limits of our environment would be defined by the span of our arms or legs. If we had acute hearing like a bat, we might understand the geometries of volumes and the extent of distance, but we would lack the ability to differentiate colors, transparencies, and textures. Sense of smell alone would be insufficient to generate a complete understanding of our surrounding environment and of

**1.3** Illuminance and perceived depth in layered space: Illuminance levels at varied distances can alter one's perception of depth in space. High illuminance levels occurring at a great distance heighten the perceived depth of a space (top), lack of illuminance variation visually flattens one's perception of space (middle), and high illuminance levels at close distances compress the apparent depth of a space (bottom).

the forms and geometries that define it. But light and vision create an internal world of distances and depth, of colors and contrasts, of volumes and textures that the majority of us inhabit.

We are all familiar with the need and desire to control light levels in accordance with our daily activities: to read, we might turn on a lamp over our book; to sleep, we might retreat to darkness; and to dine, we light a candle to establish a mood while providing sufficient light to view our food. In essence, by adjusting our light levels with a switch, a strike of a match, or a change of environment, we are controlling the visual property of illuminance to suit our programmatic needs. Likewise, the quantitative aspect of lighting design calls for differing levels of illuminance to accommodate varying activities in different spaces. Preliminary recommendations for illuminance levels in accordance to program can be found in manuals and guides issued by the Illuminating Engineering Society of North America (IESNA), a publisher of lighting design and illumination standards . For example, the IESNA calls for illuminance levels of 200 lux for incidental use, 300 lux for general office use, 500 to 700 lux for task lighting, and 1,000 to 1,500 lux for highly specialized work such as sewing, color comparison, or electronic assembly. By comparison, the midday sun provides about 32,000 to 100,000 lux depending on latitude, time of year, and cloud cover. These numbers, however, are not to be taken as absolutes, but should be considered as a guide from which a lighting designer can deduce necessary illuminance levels. Oftentimes it is advantageous to use lower light levels than convention demands.

The absence of light is also a very powerful tool. In diminished light, the physiological response of our eyes changes in order to process lower light levels, and thus what we perceive truly undergoes a visual transformation. The retina, the neural layer of our eye, houses two types of photoreceptor

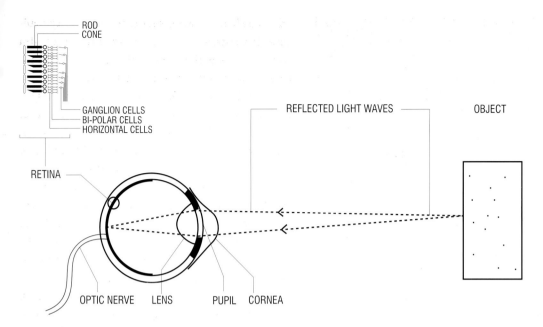

ROD
CONE

GANGLION CELLS
BI-POLAR CELLS
HORIZONTAL CELLS

RETINA

REFLECTED LIGHT WAVES        OBJECT

OPTIC NERVE     LENS     PUPIL    CORNEA

**1.4** Anatomy of the human eye

cells—rods and cones—that process different intensities and wavelengths of light into neural signals, sorted into images by the brain. 1.4 Rods are sensitive to changes in light intensity, while cones, which work best in bright light, are sensitive to color. As light levels shift, the respective activity of the rod and cone photoreceptors changes accordingly. For example, when bright light levels shift to darkness, the rods gradually take over for the cones in processing vision. As a result, the images we see in low light differ from those we might see in bright light, in that they lack the color and visual resolution facilitated by the cones, but gain a level of low-light visibility facilitated by the rods. Thus in darkness, as our eyes grow accustomed to low light levels, we discover in the shadows new visual relationships that redefine the ways in which we perceive our surroundings.

In Japanese writer Jun'ichirō Tanizaki's 1933 short essay "In Praise of Shadows," he describes the aesthetics of Japanese culture in terms of the subtlety of light and the heightened presence of shadows,

**1.5** Inside an old house in Japan: Low illuminance levels admitted through screens create an environment of both sharp and soft shadows, atmospheric light, and subtly illuminated objects.

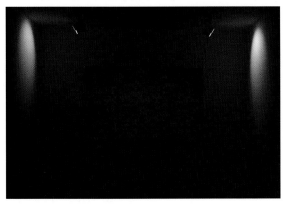

**1.6** James Turrell's *Danaë* (1983) is a permanent installation at the Mattress Factory in Pittsburgh, Pennsylvania, made with drywall, paint, and ultraviolet and incandescent light.

which he believes are essential to the country's culture. His observations on the ways in which dim lighting reveals the essence of a material, its delicate textures, nuanced form, and weathered patina beautifully illustrate how some objects and spaces are best seen and understood in the presence of feeble light and shadows. 1.5 A contemporary artist whose work also engages the eye's sensitivity to low light levels is James Turrell. In pieces such as *Danaë* (1983), Turrell casts projections of light into environments of darkness to create transformative spaces of great depth. The full extent of such a space is not immediately visible, but is instead revealed in the time required for the eye to adjust to the dim light levels of the surrounding environment. 1.6

The concept that in darkness one gains an alternative understanding of an object or space, its beauty revealed through the absence of light, is one that we as human beings can experience on a daily basis with the natural cycle of day and night. At night, when the sun has disappeared beyond the horizon, the stars and moon become visible and only then do we gain an understanding of our placement in this greater universe. However, by overlighting at night one creates a veil that diminishes this connection. 1.7a and 1.7b The proliferation of urban centers and the subsequent production of excessive light have challenged the ways in which we view the nocturnal sky. For many people around the world, the stars are most often invisible, overpowered by a mist of artificial light, the glare of street lamps, or the shimmering light of skyscrapers. Light pollution and the resultant loss of view of the nocturnal sky is of great concern to scientists and people who study the relationships of nature and the urban environment. Organizations such as the International Dark Sky Association (founded in 1988) have emerged to advocate for the reduction of unnecessary illuminance and the promotion of darkness for psychological, ecological, and aesthetic well-being.

**1.7a and 1.7b** Photographs taken near Toronto in August 2003 show the night sky during a blackout (left) and on a night with electrical power restored (right).

Likewise, in architectural environments, light can provide welcomed visibility, but it can also overstimulate or blind. The careful control of illuminance levels across spatial trajectories is crucial in ensuring visual and spatial continuity, comfort, and one's ability to see. For example, many have experienced the disorienting sensation that results when one is abruptly forced to emerge from a dark space into bright sunlight or the harsh glare of electric lighting. In designing such spatial trajectories, from extreme darkness to light, it is advantageous to slowly increase the lighting levels—from interior to exit corridor to building foyer to, finally, the outdoor space—to allow the visitor to comfortably adapt to the increase in light levels and the ultimate illuminance of the point of departure. 1.8 This same principle is implemented in the lighting of roadway tunnels by day in order to ensure vehicular safety: at

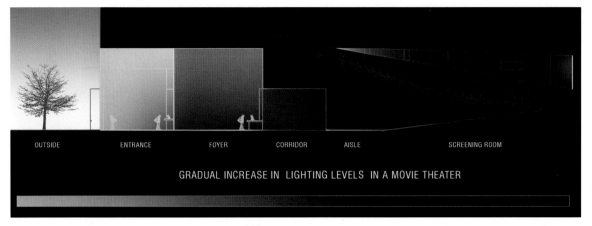

OUTSIDE    ENTRANCE    FOYER    CORRIDOR    AISLE    SCREENING ROOM

GRADUAL INCREASE IN LIGHTING LEVELS IN A MOVIE THEATER

**1.8** Gradual adjustment of lighting levels in a spatial trajectory, from bright exterior to dark interior

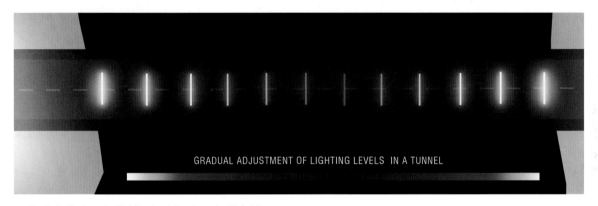

GRADUAL ADJUSTMENT OF LIGHTING LEVELS IN A TUNNEL

**1.9** Gradual adjustment of lighting levels in a tunnel, with bright lights at the entrance and exit

the entrances and exits of tunnels, bright lights are used to mediate the transition between daylight and the otherwise-darkened interior, while at the center of a tunnel, light levels can be decreased. 1.9

Obscurity, or the lack of light, can also effectively render our immediate surroundings and environments in unexpected ways. This concept is perhaps best illustrated with examples from the genre of theatrical stage lighting, where the careful control of illuminance enables the stage to become a shifting, illusionary space of the imagination. In the theater, it is possible to instantaneously hide or reveal a prop or character with lighting, such that their very being is seemingly determined by the presence or absence of light. Similarly, backdrops and scrims activated

**1.10** Layers of space are hidden and revealed through the use of lights and scrims in theater productions.

through light or the lack thereof can become visible or invisible layers that alter the depth and composition of the stage throughout the course of a performance. 1.10 In architectural design, controlled illuminance can similarly disguise and reveal layers of a facade or interior. Contemporary buildings, whose multi-layered facades offer up varying degrees of transparency, are excellent candidates for the play of light and shadow and the revelation or negation of intermediary space and substructural elements. Through the careful control of illuminance, a building can be transformed into a changing entity where different features are hidden and revealed, depending on programmatic or aesthetic requirements. 1.11a – 1.11d

We are often quick to assume that the presence of light expands, while its absence constricts, space. In reality, the relationships between light and dark and the ways in which they alter one's perception of space are far more complex. Architecture historian Steen Eiler Rasmussen describes the interchangeable nature of light and dark and their ability to evoke both solid and void as follows: "Light alone can [also] create the effect of an enclosed space. A campfire on a dark night forms a cave of light circumscribed by a wall of darkness."[1] With these words Rasmussen illustrates the didactic quality of light and dark, as they embody both the presence and absence of form, the material and immaterial. Because light is capable of representing both concrete form and atmospheric space, light and architectural elements can be used in tandem to determine the limits of a perceived space. Light can suggest the presence of limitless expanses or definitive borders, transparent openings or opaque enclosures, and dark can act as a counterpoint to light, rendering it all the more material or, conversely, all the more ephemeral. Together with built form, light and dark and the gradients in between them are a powerful palette that can further construct our understanding of an architectural space.

this page

Kohn Pedersen Fox (architect) and L'Observatoire International (lighting design), proposal for
New York Sports and Convention Center, New York, New York, 2004

**1.11a** View of building in idle mode: Orange light at its base causes the glass facade to appear
to float, and no direct light is employed behind it so that it reflects the water of the river.

**1.11c** Section through the building
facade in idle mode: Downlight
with no cast shadows

**1.11b** View of building in convention mode: Structure is exposed through the glass facade,
and the building is visually grounded by its base and facade lighting.

**1.11d** Section through the building
facade in convention mode:
Horizontal lighting projects
shadows and reveals structure.

# Reassurance

Since the beginning of time, human beings' relationship with darkness has been one fraught with tension as we grapple to celebrate the beauty and necessity of this natural condition despite its often-overwhelming presence. While darkness itself does not threaten, it can harbor the wildest creatures of one's imagination: demons, enemies, and most frightening of all, the unknown. These haunting fears often manifest themselves in the nightmares of children, overriding logical reason. Darkness, while not inherently evil, undeniably conceals—within darkness, we lose our bearings and our grasp of what surrounds us. As adults we often harbor a lingering memory of our childhood phobias and a wariness of the realities that might lurk in darkness, and thus we light candles for comfort, turn on lights when we arrive home late at night, or gravitate toward illuminated areas in large, cavernous rooms.

The correlation between darkness, reassurance, and safety is one that has been carefully examined in studies of the urban environment, often producing mixed results. Historically, the implementation of streetwide lighting systems in urban centers was intended to promote both increased vision and safety at night. Public lighting was first mandated in fifteenth-century London, and the city of Paris soon followed suit, ordering all residents whose windows faced the streets to hang lanterns at night even in the presence of the light of a full moon. The visibility promised by artificial light quickly became a desired standard despite the ongoing fear that open flames could prove to be a fire hazard. The invention of the gas lantern in the nineteenth century heralded a new age of public light, and the rhythmic flicker of gas lamps became a familiar sight along the boulevards of Paris, the avenues of London, and the cobblestone streets of Philadelphia.

Later, the discovery of electricity and the subsequent production and installment of safe and inexpensive incandescent lamps finally erased concern of fires, further promoting the prolific use of street lamps in both urban and suburban contexts. In areas that had been accustomed to the darkness of night, streetwide lighting systems were implemented for visibility and as a deterrent to criminal activity. A survey of street crimes in the records of the Cleveland, Ohio, police department in the early part of the twentieth century proved a 41 percent decrease in crime in the business district once high-illuminance ornamental lighting was installed.[2]

Today our understanding of the role of public light in urban centers continues to be based on ideas of visibility, safety, and aesthetics, but the concept of safety extends well beyond the prevention of criminal activity. We rely on light to provide uniform vision for drivers, to allow for the safe coexistence of pedestrians and automobiles on a road, and to give psychological assurance by ensuring vision to people who traverse a city by night. However, the direct relationship between the presence of light and decreased crime levels is no longer assumed to be a given.

A study conducted first in 1977 and again in 1997 by the National Institute of Justice proved that the correlation between lighting and crime is inconclusive, as many crimes are committed during daylight or in empty lit buildings by night.[3] Another study, published in 2003 by B. A. J. Clark at the Astronomical Society of Victoria Inc., Australia, went further to suggest that nighttime crime was perhaps more likely to take place in areas of high outdoor ambient-light levels, as "excessive outdoor lighting appears to facilitate some of the social factors that lead to crime."[4] This study found that areas of too much light and glare often create pockets of great contrast and deep shadows, where criminals may lurk unseen. Furthermore, the presence of great expanses of light might actually facilitate illicit activities in areas that would be otherwise deserted. Of course, in different socioeconomic environments the presence of public lighting can have drastically different effects, and none of the studies mentioned argue for the elimination of public lighting, but simply ask for the responsible use of the resource. Ultimately it is most important to light public spaces in a manner that both appears to, and actually does, keep people safe.

# Conservation

It is a beautiful paradox that light, the ephemeral and intangible substance that we rely on to shape our views of the world, also has the power of provoking extreme violence upon the same subject it brings into being. Plants that depend on the sun's ultraviolet rays for nourishment and growth simultaneously are at its mercy should these rays become too strong. Likewise, while we humans require regular sun exposure for our psychological and physical well-being, we have all experienced the excruciating pain of a sunburn or the blinding light of a high summer sun, and as a species we have developed ways to protect ourselves from excessive light exposure. The harmful effects of light are a function of intensity and exposure, and these variables must be controlled to prevent damage to the artifacts and materials of our everyday life, as well as those in specialized conditions.

It is important to remember that light is by definition energy, and that it can have an adverse effect on material it encounters. When light hits an object, a portion of the light waves is reflected and another portion is absorbed by the materiality of the object itself. The reflected light waves are the ones that reach our eyes and that we process into an image of the object. The absorbed light waves are not visible, but are potentially dangerous, causing irreversible damage to the materiality of the object. 1.12 We are all familiar with the yellowing of a carpet or the fading of a textile pattern caused by prolonged sun exposure. This damage can be limited by the control of light levels, an object's exposure to these light levels, and the minimization of ultraviolet and infrared radiation in the light emitted.

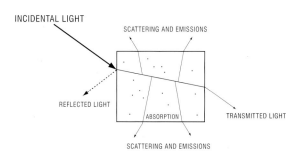

INCIDENTAL LIGHT

SCATTERING AND EMISSIONS

REFLECTED LIGHT

ABSORPTION

TRANSMITTED LIGHT

SCATTERING AND EMISSIONS

**1.12** Light can be reflected, absorbed, or transmitted by a given material. A single object can selectively reflect a wavelength of a given frequency while absorbing or transmitting others. Reflected light is what renders a surface visible. The more light reflected, the brighter the surface, and the more light absorbed, the darker it appears. A surface that transmits some light appears transparent.

Visible light resides between the ultraviolet and infrared regions of the electromagnetic spectrum. 1.13 While ultraviolet and infrared waves are invisible to the human eye, they are nonetheless damaging and present in many types of light. Daylight contains ultraviolet, visible, and infrared wavelengths of light, while various artificial light sources contain a combination of two or three of these wavelengths—thus, light must be filtered and controlled to prove safe.

As lighting designers, we are responsible for completing studies of how light will interact and be distributed within a given space. These calculations ensure that illuminance levels will be sufficient for comfort and visibility and nondamaging to the objects and materials in the space. Museum exhibition design is an area where carefully calculated illuminance is essential to the protection of objects. Light that is not properly controlled or filtered may cause both photochemical damage (fading) and photomechanical damage (degradation) to an object or material. The exhibition of valued artifacts calls for precise illuminance levels that address both the specificity of material and the amount of time the artifact will be on view. Because the preservation of an artifact is dependent on both illuminance levels

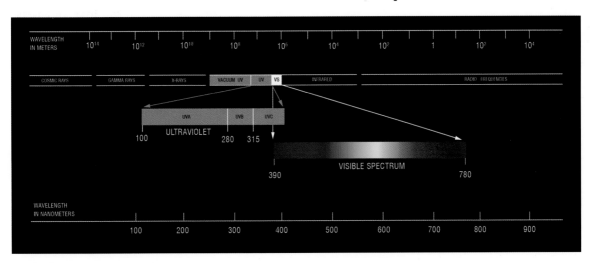

**1.13** The electromagnetic spectrum

and time of exposure, lux levels can be increased if lux hours are restrained, and vice-versa. The illuminance of a museum exhibition or any other interior can be achieved through a combination of natural and electric light, but the use of appropriate filters and controlled light levels is essential to the care and preservation of the objects within.

# Light Energy

Conservation is not just a subject concerning the preservation of materials and objects, but a notion equally relevant to the use of light itself. Today, a pervading awareness of the fragility of our natural resources and of the importance of energy conservation in ensuring the preservation of our natural environments and the sustainability of modern living standards are prevalent in the lighting design community. The future conservation of light energy is dependent on both advances in lighting technologies and on our meaningful and responsible use of lighting in the built environment.

Recent advances in technical aspects of lighting design have allowed the industry to make headway in the quest to become more energy efficient. In particular, the great array of light fixtures and technologies now available for public use allows the consumer to opt for more energy-efficient lighting than was available in the past. Several factors that are commonly considered when selecting a luminaire (the term for a complete lighting unit) include source efficacy (the amount of energy consumed versus the amount of light emitted measured in lumens per watt), life span of the source, cost (initial cost versus long-term savings), quality of light emitted, and the sustainability of processes and materials used in manufacturing. (A comparison of basic properties of different light technologies can be found in Appendix D, p. 137.) Recent campaigns encouraging consumers to replace incandescent bulbs with compact fluorescents are one example of the industry's push to educate the public about energy-conscious lighting. While a standard incandescent bulb has an efficacy of 15 to 20 lumens per watt and a life span of approximately 750 to 1,000 hours, a compact fluorescent lamp has an efficacy of 60 to 100 lumens per watt and a life span of 12,000 hours or more, and is thus the energy-conscious choice for consumers.[5] In the past, people were often hesitant to use fluorescent bulbs in their homes for fear of the harsh, cold light they might emit, but in recent years advances in technology have greatly improved the color and color-rendering abilities of fluorescent lamps, and the aesthetic qualities of the light emitted are now more similar to those of an incandescent bulb. As with most technologies, though, there are both positive and negative aspects to be considered with the development of new forms of electric lighting. While compact fluorescent lamps are incredibly energy efficient, each lamp contains a small amount of mercury that can contaminate the environment if improperly disposed of. Light-emitting diode (LED) lamps provide an environmentally safe alternative to compact fluorescents, and their life span supersedes both that of incandescent and compact fluorescent bulbs (a typical LED has a lifespan of fifty-thousand hours). However, the color-rendering abilities of LEDs are not yet comparable to those of compact fluorescent or incandescent lamps. As new lighting technologies are continuously developed and existing ones improved, factors such as cost, quality of light, life span, and energy efficacy will surely drive the industry's innovations.

Other technical advances that facilitate the conservation of light energy today include lighting control systems—such as dimmers, photocells, occupation sensors, and time-clock scheduling—to prevent light from being wasted when it is not needed. Dimmers allow users to adjust light levels of a grouping of similar source types depending on the time of day and programmatic demands of a space. Photocells are instruments used to sense daylight levels, allowing electric light to increase or decrease in accordance to the patterns of natural light. Occupancy sensors simply detect movement in a space, enabling lights to be automatically turned on when a person is present and turned off in their absence. Time-clock scheduling may be programmed to turn lights on and off in accordance to a predetermined schedule. A lighting control system further facilitates the management of different lighting control devices. The use of such systems can save 20 percent to 50 percent of a building's lighting power consumption while reducing environmental impacts associated with excessive energy use. In large-scale building programs, a lighting system can be integrated into the building management system (BMS)—a computer-run, building-wide system that monitors and controls the environment within— for increased operational benefits.

While technical advances are crucial in the quest to conserve energy, responsible use of light is a fundamental means by which great change can be made. Conservation of light energy can be as simple as turning lights off when a room or a building is not in use. However, objectivity and the ability to constantly question and re-evaluate standards of light use are perhaps a lighting designer's most powerful tools in ensuring responsible use of light from the first stages of schematic design to user occupancy. Oftentimes it is best to ask not how much light is necessary to render a space functional, but how little light can be put to use for maximum effect. For example, while the IESNA lighting design guide suggests illuminance levels of 300 lux in an office environment, it is important to realize that these 300 lux are necessary only for the task surfaces, not the entire space. By designing for 100 lux in circulation areas, one can lower energy consumption by approximately 65 percent, while simultaneously creating spatial hierarchy and visual interest. While it is not always easy to challenge convention, innovation is not achieved without experimentation and risk. The conservation of energy is a subject that will only become more pressing in the coming years, and lighting designers' responsibility to maximize the effects of light while minimizing the consumption of energy will surely continue to drive and influence the aesthetic and direction of our work in the future.

1   Steen Eiler Rasmussen, *Experiencing Architecture* (Cambridge, MA: MIT Press, 1986), 208–9.

2   O. F. Haas, "Planning the Street Lighting System," *Planning for City Traffic: Annals of the American Academy of Political and Social Science* 133 (Sept. 1927): 34–49.

3   International Dark Sky Association, "Light Pollution and Safety" (2008), http://docs.darksky.org/Docs/ida_safety_brochure.pdf.

4   B. A. J. Clark, "Outdoor Lighting and Crime, Part 2: Coupled Growth" (Victoria: Astronomical Society of Australia, 2003), 1. http://amper.ped.muni.cz/light/crime/OLCpt2.htm.

5   Numbers are estimated in accordance to General Electric specifications on standard incandescent and compact fluorescent lightbulbs.

# Luminance

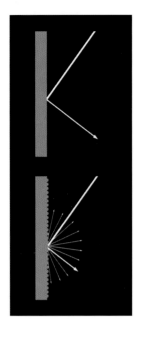

**2.1** Surface texture and reflection: A specular surface will reflect light in a singular direction at an angle equal to its angle of incidence, while a matte surface will disperse light in a multitude of directions and, as a result, appear more diffuse.

Light is reflected back to the human eye at the interface of two different materials. The relative brightness of this perceived light is dependent on the physical properties of the reflective material. A smooth, mirrorlike surface will reflect unobstructed light waves—where the angle of incidence is equal to the angle of reflection, creating a focused light—while a textured surface will reflect light waves from various angles of incidence, creating the illusion of a brighter, multidirectional light. 2.1 The visual property of luminance aims to explain this phenomenon, quantifying the intensity of emitted light from a given surface. Luminance is measured in footlambert or candela per square meter. Luminance ratios describe the difference in brightness between two objects or areas in a given environment. Juxtapositions of luminance levels and employment of varied contrast can be used to give a sense of hierarchy and direction to space through light.

## Light, Reflection, and Material

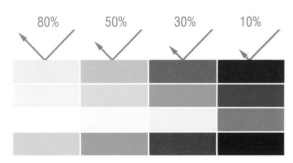

**2.2** Value and reflectivity: A light color will reflect a greater percentage of incoming light waves, while a dark color will reflect a lesser percentage of incoming light waves, absorbing the rest.

Luminance and brightness are two concepts that go hand in hand, though they are often confused with each other. While luminance is the objective measure of light intensity per unit area, brightness is the subjective sensation that we, the viewer, experience when looking at an object or surface. A surface of high luminosity will most often appear bright while one of low luminosity will appear dark. Because a surface's material properties affect the way in which light waves are reflected back to the eye, the concept of luminance in lighting design is inextricably linked to built form, materiality, and color. 2.2 For example, a lamp shining on a white wall will produce a light of higher luminance than the same lamp shining on a black wall, although the perceived contrast will be less on the white wall than on the black wall. 2.3 and 2.4 Similarly, a lamp shining on a matte-finish white wall will produce

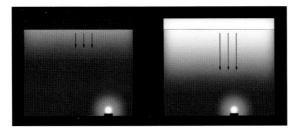

**2.3** Luminance comparison of a black wall and a white wall: A lamp shining on a white wall will produce a light of greater luminance than the same light shining on a dark wall because the white paint will reflect most incoming light waves, while the black paint absorbs them.

**2.4** Luminance versus contrast for a black wall and a white wall: While luminance values are greater for a lamp shining on a white wall, visual contrast is higher for the same light shining on the black wall.

**2.5** Luminance perceived from a hidden light source

a light of higher luminance than one shining on a glossy-finish white wall because the uneven surface of the matte wall will better disperse the light in a multitude of directions than that of the glossy finish. A lighting designer must take into consideration the surface finishes and textures of the space and objects that he wishes to illuminate, as these materials are capable of augmenting or negating the light of a luminaire, and in turn may potentially appear themselves as sources of reflected light.

Perhaps one of the most surprising yet powerful ideas in lighting design is that a surface or object itself has the potential to become a secondary light source. Consider the moon: it does not emit light on its own, but the sun's light reflected off the moon's surface creates what we recognize as moonlight. Similarly, a wall or other architectural element has the capacity to reflect light, thus becoming a light source of its own in a given space. Oftentimes a light fixture will be recessed into a ceiling cove and hidden from view, making it seem that the sole source of light is the wall or object that the initial light beams shine upon. 2.5

There is something magical about a luminous surface that embodies light reflected from a disguised source. In Byzantine icon paintings, the golden halo above the head of a religious figure appears to glow from within as a symbol of the divine. While the gold leaf of the halo itself reflects light to the human eye, the original light source—be it ambient daylight or flickering candles—goes unnoticed in the dark church setting. Furthermore, the contrast between the brightness of the halo against the dark painted flesh of a saint's face reveals the figure in silhouette, heightening the mystery of this seemingly divine light.

In contemporary architecture, indirect lighting and luminous surfaces continue to invoke a sense of the unexpected in both ecclesiastic and secular settings. For example, Eero Saarinen's chapel

Eero Saarinen, Massachusetts Institute of Technology Chapel, Cambridge, Massachusetts, 1955

**2.7** Chapel interior: Light reflected from the exterior moat illuminates the undulating brick walls of the interior chapel.

**2.6** Exterior of the chapel, with moat

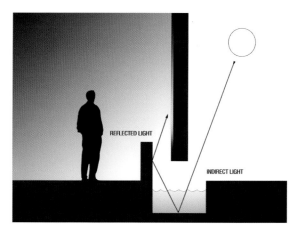

REFLECTED LIGHT

INDIRECT LIGHT

**2.8** Diagram of indirect and reflected light in the chapel

Steven Holl Architects and L'Observatoire International (lighting design), Chapel of Saint Ignatius, Seattle University, Seattle, Washington, 1995

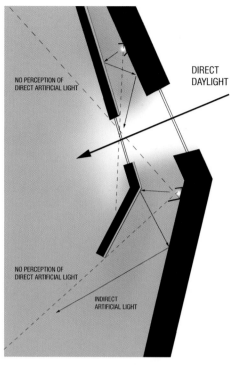

**2.10** Diagram of the chapel's direct and indirect lighting

**2.9** View of typical window/wall construction in the chapel's interior, where natural and electric light emanate from behind the colored walls: The white light reflected off the colored wall surface emerges as colored light in the space due to subtractive absorption.

at the Massachusetts Institute of Technology in Cambridge (1955) succeeds in channeling natural daylight reflected off the building's surrounding moat into the cylindrical brick perimeter of the interior chapel, to phenomenal effect. 2.6 – 2.8 The color, direction, and intensity of the sunlight and the motion, patterns, and transparency of the water are projected onto the interior walls, where light waves dance upon the undulating surface of brick. Likewise, much of architect Steven Holl's work experiments with the experiential potential of luminous surfaces as light sources in a wide range of programmatic spaces. Holl's signature use of colored light emerging from behind a planar surface again exemplifies how light can be transformed by the surface with which it interacts. 2.9 and 2.10 In Holl's case, a light directed on a colored, luminous surface disguised behind a wall or ceiling reflects soft halos of colored light into a space. This indirect light is a mere whisper of the light source and colored surface from which it emerges. Such careful orchestrations of light, material, and color illustrate the power of luminance to transform the ways in which we experience a space.

## Contrast and Hierarchy

**2.11** Shawn Hausman (interior designer) and L'Observatoire International (lighting design), The Standard Hotel, Los Angeles, California, 2003: Silhouette of a topiary figure before a lit wall

The human eye is invariably drawn to light. Our eyes are accustomed to scanning our environments, fixating on areas of brightness that most often capture our gaze. However, an area of high luminosity only appears bright if it is surrounded by an area of low luminosity. Thus contrast—the juxtaposition of light with its counterpart, darkness—is necessary for us to distinguish foreground from background, positive from negative, architectural form from space.

Because luminance is the measure of light emitted over a given surface area, material adjacencies should exhibit luminance contrast in order to read independently from one another. Two surfaces with similar luminance levels will visually meld together and read as one, while articulation of different luminance levels on these surfaces will accentuate their individual form, establishing a distinct spatial relationship between one and the other. The silhouette of a figure before a lit wall is a strong example of the heightened reading of form that high-luminance contrast can produce. 2.11

While luminance contrast is capable of hiding or revealing form, it can also simultaneously augment or negate one's perception of depth and the reading of a space. If two identical objects are positioned side by side with one lit brightly and the other less so, the brighter object appears larger and closer, while the less bright object appears smaller and further away. By pushing luminance levels to relative

**2.12** Effects of luminance in accentuating or negating perception of depth through a window

extremes and creating areas of great contrast, one can visually alter spatial limits, creating illusions of distance and depth through the manipulation of light. Such careful control of luminance contrasts is often used in the windows of retail environments as a business strives to draw customers into a space. In order to break down the visual barrier of the store-front window, high luminance levels are employed at the back of a store to draw the eyes into the depths of the retail environment. Alternatively, if the window were to have a higher luminance level than the back wall of the store, the reflectivity of the store window would act as a visual barrier preventing one from seeing in, thus compressing the perceived limits of the space. 2.12

Differing degrees of luminance and varied relationships of brightness and darkness are also crucial in establishing hierarchy within a space. The careful choreography of bright and dark can guide people's eyes and steer their passage through a space while simultaneously signaling places of importance and moments of pause in the visual or spatial trajectory. Hierarchy of luminance can be objectively controlled through the use of luminance ratios, a comparative system of numbers that describes a surface's brightness in relation to another. In typical interior spaces, luminance ratios of 10:9 or 5:4 describe uniformity in luminance, whereas a 10:1 ratio is considered dramatic. A 20:1 luminance ratio is typical of egress-path lighting in emergency situations, and ratios greater than 20:1 are often objectionable. While high contrast succeeds in capturing the viewer's attention, one must keep in mind that it is not always the optimal choice, as our minds can be jolted by such an effect and our vision can be impeded. In places such as a workstation, where the eye must navigate many surfaces at once over the course of a work period, the careful control of luminance ratios and the assurance of medium to low lighting contrast in programmatic adjacencies are essential to ensure the utmost comfort and practicality of use for the person at work.

# Glare and Sparkle

Glare, the sensation of discomfort caused when high levels of luminance are misdirected toward the eye, is a condition that lighting designers must control in their quest to create a visually tolerable and programmatically functional space. Glare is both a function of luminance area and of the lighting position within a field of view. A small surface of a given luminance may be visually acceptable, while a larger surface with the same luminance might provoke a sense of visual violence. Likewise, a fixture with a given luminance located in the periphery of one's field of view may be unobtrusive, but the same fixture at eye level can be intolerable. Glare, in addition to causing general discomfort, can also limit one's perception of space and sense of depth, acting as a visual barrier, a sort of wall that is visually difficult to trespass. For example, on a concert stage, a performer who inhabits the same physical space as his audience is often blinded by the glare of spotlights, and thus cannot see the audience for which he performs. This bifurcation of experiential space, while conceptually fascinating, can be disadvantageous and obstructive, and must be carefully monitored and controlled.

Glare also proves to be a problematic condition when it distracts from a light source's intended effect. Often, the glare of an unshielded light source within plain view can overwhelm the viewer, preventing him from seeing what the light source aims to highlight. Such unsightly lighting can often be found in city streets or parks, where bright street lamps intended to illuminate the surroundings inadvertently negate their presence. 2.13a and 2.13b A properly lit park will draw the visitor's eyes to the pedestrian walkways, plantings, and monuments, not to the light sources themselves. For this reason,

**2.13a and 2.13b** Roadway lighting without (top) and with (bottom) glare shields

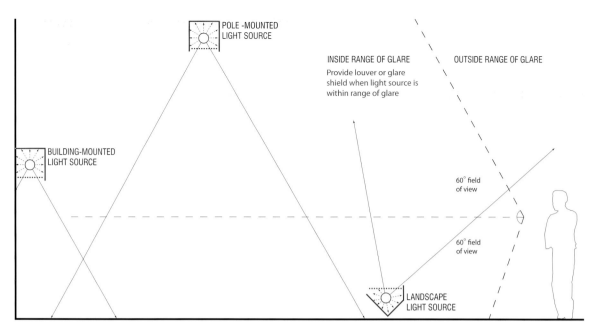

POLE-MOUNTED LIGHT SOURCE

INSIDE RANGE OF GLARE

Provide louver or glare shield when light source is within range of glare

OUTSIDE RANGE OF GLARE

BUILDING-MOUNTED LIGHT SOURCE

60° field of view

60° field of view

LANDSCAPE LIGHT SOURCE

**2.14** Glare prevention: Exterior fixtures situated within 60 degrees above eye level generally require shielding to prevent uncomfortable glare.

**2.15** Georges de la Tour, *The Education of the Virgin* (1650), oil on canvas: The young girl's hand shields the light source and acts as a reflector, permitting the viewer an intimate and unobstructed view of the scene that unfolds.

recessed fixtures, shields, and other disguises are often employed to minimize glare, enabling the human eye to focus and adapt to the visual effect of light upon the surface or object they illuminate. 2.14

Georges de la Tour's painting *The Education of the Virgin* (1650) beautifully illustrates the emotive power of a light whose source is concealed. In this work, it is the effect of light, not the light source itself that delivers the poignant message of this scene. As the girl shields the flame of the candle with her hand, she facilitates an intimate view of a scene that would otherwise be obstructed by glare. Furthermore, without the glare of the candle, the viewer can quite literally see the symbolic connection between the girl and the book: it is the book itself that truly illuminates the young girl. 2.15 A contemporary example of a light source whose symbolic effect is dependent on the physicality of its shield is the MAYUHANA lantern, designed by architect Toyo Ito. This cocoonlike luminaire produces a soft light filtered through many layers of tightly interwoven fiberglass threads. By the time

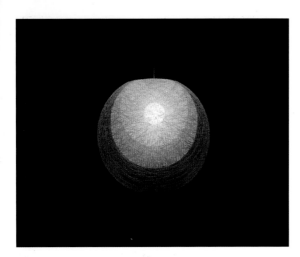

**2.16** Toyo Ito's MAYUHANA light fixture

**2.18** Transmitted sparkle from a chandelier

the light reaches the human eye, it has dissolved into the materiality of the many layers that shelter the electric source at the lantern's very core. 2.16

Of course, it would be incorrect to make a sweeping generalization that all glare or pockets of extremely bright light are detrimental to the visual experience of a space or that they should be shielded. Our tolerance for bright lights varies greatly depending on mood, ambience, necessity, and surrounding environment, and at times, pockets of brilliant light can punctuate a space in an advantageous manner. Such a positive occurrence of controlled glare is referred to as sparkle. Lighting designer Gary Gordon categorizes the occurrence of sparkle into three different typologies—direct sparkle, reflected sparkle, and transmitted sparkle—that prove useful when contextualizing the visual effects of incidents of bright light.[1] A scene demonstrating the varied effects of sparkle is captured by French photographer Léon Gimpel in his photograph *Salon d'Automne* (1903). In this black-and-white image of a Parisian night scene, the direct sparkle of little incandescent lights upon a gatewaylike structure and their reflected sparkle in the water conjure a sense of evanescent beauty. 2.17 An example of transmitted sparkle is the light embodied in the fragmented pieces of a crystal chandelier, which is further dispersed into the surrounding space by millions of small crystal facets. 2.18 Sparkle in its multitude of forms can add visual interest to a space, punctuating areas of darkness, enlivening an otherwise-still scene, or drawing attention to key spatial elements—be it a light source or a reflective surface, such as the crystal facets of a chandelier—in unexpected ways. Our sensitivity to light, darkness, and contrast provides ample opportunity for generating unique experiences, thresholds, and environments through sparkle and the careful control of luminance.

1  Gary Gordon, *Interior Lighting for Designers*, 4th ed. (Hoboken, NJ: John Wiley & Sons, 2003), 41–42.

**2.17** Direct and reflected sparkle in Léon Gimpel's photograph
*Paris, Salon d'Automne* (1903)

# Color and Temperature

The color of light is inextricably linked to perception of space and time. Very often, we do not remember the architectural details of a space, but rather the cool blue light of a winter morning or the warm glow of a setting sun is what lingers in our memories, shaping our understanding of a space inhabited at a precise time. Light color alters the way in which we perceive objects and their surroundings. It has the power to transform the familiar into the exotic, rendering new relationships and chromatic contrasts between foreground and background, form and atmosphere. Because every object obtains its colored appearance in part from the light it absorbs or reflects, light color can transform our perception of an object and its surroundings such that new spatial, formal, or chromatic relationships are discovered.

## Technical Measure: Wavelength, Color Temperature, and the Color Rendering Index

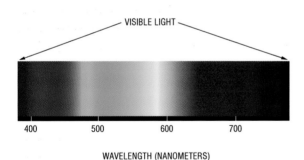

VISIBLE LIGHT

400　　　500　　　600　　　700

WAVELENGTH (NANOMETERS)

**3.1** Electromagnetic spectrum: visible light

Our perception of color is determined by both the physical properties of light and the human body's physiological and psychological response to the light that enters the eye. Light by definition is a type of electromagnetic radiation that is emitted when charged particles, or photons, move. This energy, which is characterized by its frequency of wavelength, is part of a greater continuous range of radiation called the electromagnetic spectrum. Visible light is simply the portion of this spectrum whose wavelengths are recognized and processed by receptors in our eyes. What we perceive as visible light is defined as the range of wavelengths that fall between ultraviolet and infrared radiation, between 380 and 780 nanometers. 3.1 Colors within this visible spectrum are distinguished by either a single wavelength or a range of wavelengths. Colors that can be defined by a single wavelength are called pure spectral, or monochromatic, colors, and are labeled by hue: red, orange, yellow, green, blue, and purple. However, the majority of the colors we see are actually composed of a range of wavelengths, and white light is the combination of many visible wavelengths mixed together.

Because white light is emitted in a multitude of wavelengths that together determine the perceived coloration, the notion of color temperature in lighting design is used to further describe a light's visual qualities. Color temperature is the *visual* appearance of a white light emitted by a given source, which can range in color from warm hues (reddish) to cool hues (bluish). Numerically, the color temperature of a light source—measured in Kelvin (k)—refers to the quantity of energy, or heat, required to render a blackbody radiator a visible color. In scientific terms, a blackbody radiator is an imaginary object that absorbs all electromagnetic radiation, rendering it black. While this idea may seem somewhat abstract and difficult to grasp, the concept can be more easily understood when we substitute the notion of a blackbody radiator with that of a bar of steel. When a steel bar is subject to heat, it will begin to emit different colors of light: at low temperatures a steel bar will glow a fiery red, and as temperatures increase it will start to glow a pale yellow, then white, then a pale blue and ultimately, brilliant blue. Likewise, the Kelvin scale for color temperature of light sources ranges from reds (1,500k–2,000k) to yellows (2,500k–3,000k) to whites (3,000–4,000k) to pale blues (4,000k–6,500k) and then sky blues (6,500k and higher)—the higher the Kelvin temperature, the cooler the color hue. The fact that reddish hues are referred to as warm color and bluish hues as cool color is simply due to the cultural connotation that red equals heat (fire) and blue equals cold (snow and ice).

Electric lighting technologies have the capacity to produce white light of varying color temperatures through combinations of different wavelengths on the color spectrum. Spectral energy-distribution graphs visually depict the range and intensities of wavelengths emitted by a given light source, and

**3.2a - 3.2f** Spectral energy-distribution graphs illustrating the intensity and range of wavelengths emitted by a given light source: Natural daylight and incandescent light emit energy in a continuous spectrum of wavelengths, while other man-made sources emit light whose energy spectrum is characterized by discontinuous peaks of wavelengths of a given frequency (images courtesy of General Electric Company).

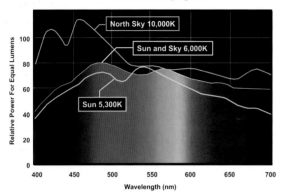

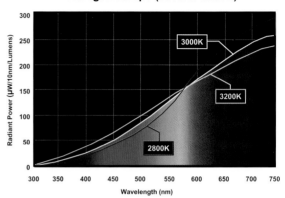

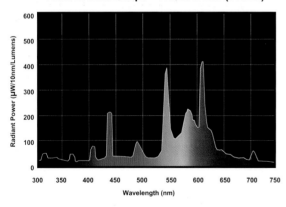

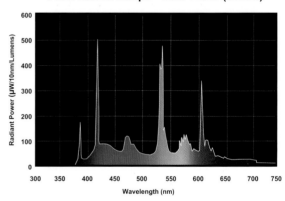

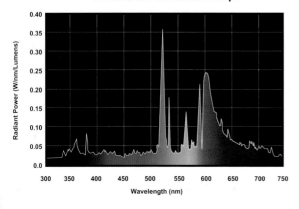

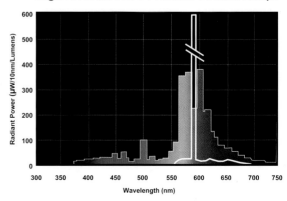

the comparison of such graphs demonstrates diversity of colors emitted by different technolc g----

3.2a–3.2f Natural and incandescent light sources both emit light continuously across the color spectrum, while fluorescent, LED, and high-intensity discharge lamps emit light in concentrated peaks within the spectrum. These peaks combine to give the impression of white light, for which a color temperature can be measured. An illustrative graph depicting the approximate color temperatures of different light sources can be found in Appendix C (p. 136).

While the estimation of color temperature qualifies a light's overall visual tendency toward warm or cool hues, it fails to address the ways in which it renders colors. For example, while a fluorescent lamp and an incandescent lamp might emit light of the same color temperature, the manner in which they render color vastly differs because the light frequencies emitted by an incandescent source are continuous on the color spectrum, while those emitted by a fluorescent source are discontinuous, with peaks and absences of frequencies. To address this discrepancy, a rating system called the color rendering index (CRI)—which ranges in value from 1 to 100—quantifies a light source's ability to render a series of colors true to an established reference source. CRIs are only comparable for sources of the same color temperature, and as a rule of thumb, sources with higher CRIs (80–100) make subjects look more natural than sources with lower CRIs. A depictive illustration of colors rendered by light sources of differing CRI values further exemplifies this point. 3.3

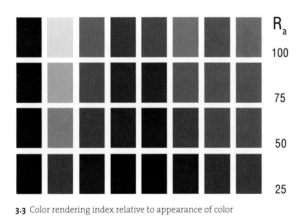

$R_a$

100

75

50

25

**3.3** Color rendering index relative to appearance of color

## Visual Impressions

While wavelength, color temperature, and the color rendering index are technical measures used to describe the quality and color of light, a more subjective and perhaps familiar language of color terminology is also used in order to further describe lighting's different chromatic effects. When describing colors

**3.4** Color wheel illustrating the relationship between properties of hue and saturation

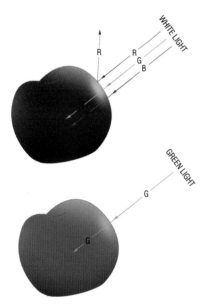

**3.5** Color appearance: Absorbance and reflection of light waves on a red apple

colloquially, we primarily speak in a language of hue, lightness, and saturation. Hue is an adjective that describes the trait we commonly recognize as color (red, yellow, green, blue, and purple), lightness refers to a color's subjective brightness (light blue versus dark blue), while saturation refers to the color's purity or intensity against a counterpoint of gray. 3.4 These three visual properties of color are equally important, along with the measure of color temperature, in allowing one to describe, recognize, and create a given experience and atmosphere through the use of light color.

Our perception of color in our surrounding environments, however, is not solely defined by the quality of light emitted by a given source, but also by an object or surface's ability to reflect or transmit such light. For example, an apple appears red when illuminated by white light because it transmits light in the frequency of red wavelengths while absorbing those in other parts of the spectrum. If this same apple is illuminated solely with green light, it will appear dark gray, as there are no red light waves to reflect and all other light waves are absorbed. 3.5 Thus it is essential to consider both the color of light emitted by a given source as well as the qualities of its surrounding environment when determining the eventual color of a given space.

The ability to render colored surfaces through the use of colored light is fundamental to the art of lighting design. For example, consider the simple task of lighting a painted red wall. The paint of the red wall is a chemical or pigment that selectively absorbs most wavelengths in the electromagnetic spectrum while reflecting those that fall within the red frequencies. Using the same logic illustrated in the lighting of the apple, if the red wall is lit with white light, it will appear red, but a dull red, as there are few red wavelengths to reflect. If this same wall is lit with red light, it will appear a brighter and more luminous red, as there is a higher quantity

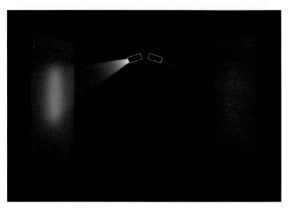

**3.6** Illumination of red wall with white light (left) and red light (right)

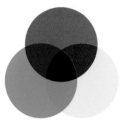

**3.7** Subtractive color mixing

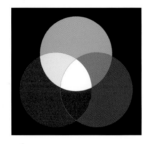

**3.8** Additive color mixing

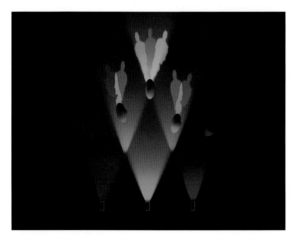

**3.9** Chromatic shadows

of light waves falling within the red portion of the light spectrum to reflect. 3.6 By carefully choosing the color temperature of the light with which one illuminates a given surface, the color intensity and hue of this surface can be altered and the desired experiential effect achieved.

While light's interaction with a material is crucial to rendering color, its interaction with other light can also produce an exciting array of colors, as well as a diverse palette of experiential and architectural possibilities. In order to understand the subsequent effects of mixing light, it is critical to realize that the color we perceive as black is in essence the absence of light waves, while the color we perceive as white is the presence of many light waves in the visible portion of the electromagnetic spectrum. When mixing light one is essentially adding light waves, and thus the more colors that are combined together, the more the light will tend toward the color white. In this sense, mixing light colors differs from mixing pigment colors because light obeys the rules of additive mixing, while pigments obey the rules of subtractive mixing. When mixing pigments, the three primary colors are cyan, magenta, and yellow, and the mixture of all three colors yields black. 3.7 However, when mixing light, the three primary colors are red, green, and blue, and the mixture of all three colors yields white. 3.8 With light, the overlap of two sources generally yields a lighter and brighter color, while the elimination of a particular spectrum of wavelengths in white light yields a darker-colored light.

Due to the principle of additive mixing in lighting, shadows are often inherently colored. These colored, or chromatic, shadows result when a particular range of wavelengths are blocked from white light. 3.9 When the impressionist artists of the nineteenth century painted their world in dazzling colored strokes, there was much visual truth in their rendering of shadows, composed of different hues

**3.10** Claude Monet, *Stacks of Wheat (Sunset, Snow Effect)* (1890/91), oil on canvas

**3.11** Georges-Pierre Seurat, study for *A Sunday on La Grande Jatte* (1884–85), oil on canvas

## Identity through Color

of blue, purple, pink, and scarlet. Claude Monet's haystacks reflect the golden rays of the setting sun, casting deep shadows of blue and lavender on the ground on which they sit. 3.10 The pointillist creations of Georges-Pierre Seurat provide a sort of didactic visual explanation of the scientific phenomena that white light is in truth composed of infinite color. The optical blending of little dots of various paint colors gives the viewer an impression of a white cloud, a purple dress, or green grass. 3.11 This rendering of chromatic light and shadow, realized in impressionist paintings, has continued to be a subject of interest further explored in the world of contemporary art. Light artists like Dan Flavin have continued to experiment with the potential of colored light and shadows and the ways in which they might alter our perception of space on a greater architectural scale. Flavin's minimalist sculptures, composed of fluorescent light tubes, demonstrate that colorful shadows are cast onto the walls and floors when a particular color of light is blocked, altering the aesthetic of the environment in unexpected ways. 3.12 As an architectural intervention, carefully choreographed sequences of chromatic light and shadows can provide an element of the unexpected in an otherwise traditional space.

Color in lighting design has the distinct ability to contribute identity and orientation to a place. On a large urban scale, color can be utilized in master plans as a sort of visual compass that orients the visitor within the greater site while simultaneously highlighting places of importance. For example, L'Observatoire International's lighting master plan proposal for the University of Puerto Rico (2005) employs light color as a wayfinding device to orient visitors. Building facades are illuminated with the color that corresponds to their cardinal orientation, and bollard lighting employed throughout the major circulation

**3.12** Dan Flavin, *Untitled (For Ksenia) #1*, Städtische Galerie im
Lenbachhaus, Munich, Germany, 2007

Field Operations (landscape design) and L'Observatoire International (lighting design), University of Puerto Rico Campus, Río Piedras Campus Master Plan, San Juan, Puerto Rico, 2005

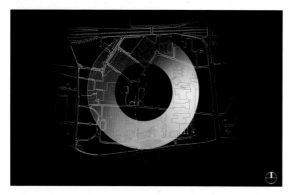

**3.13** Site plan with compass of light

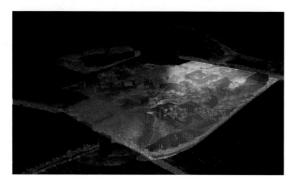

**3.14** Site rendering showing the use of colored light in establishing campus-wide visual orientation: Dark blue points north, white east, amber south, and pale blue west.

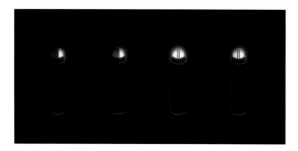

**3.15** Bollard lighting was designed to orient visitors traversing the campus by night. The white light on the bollards is positioned to face the roadway, while the colored light faces the landscape, its hue corresponding to the direction in which it points (from left to right: north, west, east, and south bollards).

routes correspondingly indicates directional axes. 3.13 – 3.15 Similarly, on a smaller building scale, color can also be used to identify spaces and programs while branding the experience with a visual cue. Colored light can leave us with lasting impressions of a place because we are apt to remember our experiences by the color in which they were rendered.

The controlled use of light colors can also intensify the experience of an environment or induce extreme emotion. It is no mystery that different colors tend to elicit different psychological responses. A large public space bathed in magenta might evoke euphoria, a sense of communal ecstasy, while a deep ultramarine blue could convey a sort of calm stillness. The careful choice and use of color in an architectural setting can shape occupants' memories and experiences of a space while provoking psychological responses in situ. However, while the psychological effects of colors have been greatly studied, and correlations between color and induced emotion developed, oftentimes the selection of color is a deeply personal decision, resulting in a subjective experience.

When colored light is used to define and possibly saturate a space, it simultaneously alters our perception of exterior spaces that are otherwise physically untouched by the application of lighting. When our eyes grow accustomed to a single hue, upon exiting that environment we perceive our surroundings in a hue complementary to the one in which we were initially immersed. This aftereffect is a result of the physiology of vision and the function of the cone photoreceptor cells in the retina. Complementary color aftereffects occur when cone cells grow fatigued from the prolonged presence of a single hue. Thus, when the cone cells are allowed to readjust to a neutral color, they are initially slow to shift from the previously processed hue, and render the new scene in a complementary hue. Likewise, when cone cells are allowed to adapt to the presence

**3.16** Interior view of the Flandres train station in Lille, France

of a single hue for an extended period of time, the brain can grow accustomed to that given color, dulling its effect. For the full intensity of the color to be truly recognized, one must provide a visual opportunity for the brain to recalibrate. In other words, the only way to experience the full effect of a color-saturated space is to ultimately look outside of it.

The aesthetic potential of saturated light colors and illusionary aftereffects can be further explained with a case study of the lighting of the Flandres train station in Lille, France. In celebration of the city's selection as the cultural capital of Europe in 2004, L'Observatoire International, with interior design firm Agence Patrick Jouin, bathed the interior of the train station in magenta light. 3.16 The train station became a glowing icon and visual symbol of the structure's radiating force, seen from all parts of the city at night. However, its visual influence

**this and previous page**

Agence Patrick Jouin (interior design) and L'Observatoire International (lighting design), Flandres Train Station, Lille, France, 2004

ultimately extended beyond the novelty of a train station glowing magenta: by bathing the interior of the train station in magenta, the surrounding environs were simultaneously "painted" a hue of blue-green, perceived by visitors upon exiting the station by means of illusionary aftereffects. 3.17 and 3.18 The

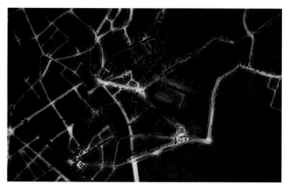

**3.17** Exterior illusionary aftereffects

**3.18** Concept plan for lighting of the train station and its visual influence on the surrounding urban context

magenta, which provided a visual counterpoint to the overcast skies and gray landscape of this industrial city, ultimately transformed the coloring of the city itself. Thus, the influence of this injected color resonated far beyond the architectural limits of the train station.

# Natural and Artificial Light

Our circadian rhythms are governed by a daily cycle of light and dark whose nuanced colors evolve with the passing of time. Over the course of the day, the sun will travel on a 180-degree arc through the sky, bathing the landscape in hues of red, orange, white, blue, pink, purple, deep red, and colors in between. We have internalized the colors and patterns of natural daylight such that we can tell the time of day and month of year by the quality of the atmospheric light.

With electric light as well as with mediated sunlight, we have the opportunity to manipulate the cycle of color and introduce other kinds of time and forms of duration. In interior lighting, it is often

**3.19** Christian Liaigre (interior architect) and L'Observatoire International (lighting design), Mercer Kitchen, New York, New York, 1998: Perimeter uplighting behind bench seating gives a sense of intimacy evocative of the setting sun.

effective to vary the color, hue, and saturation of light throughout the course of a night in order to give a sense of atmospheric movement and the passing of time. For example, behind a horizon line of perimeter bench seating, an emanating light might evolve from a soft gold to a bright crimson to a deep amber, signaling a passing of time evocative of the changing hues of a sunset. 3.19

Similarly, the selection of lighting types, their range of frequencies, and the color temperature of light they emit are essential to staging an appropriate mood and scene. Incandescent lights, whose low color temperatures are concentrated in the red-yellow range of the spectrum, and whose energy is emitted in a smooth curve of continuous wavelengths, produce a warm glow that recalls the light of the setting sun, open fires, and lit candles. Fluorescent lights—which can come in both warm and cool color temperatures, but whose energy is emitted in discontinuous peaks of singular wavelengths—are often used to create the sensation of ambient light within a space. Logically, a designer will choose a lighting source that reflects the colors of light appropriate to a given program when approaching the design of a space. For this reason we often dine by warm candlelight—an incandescent glow similar to the quality of light that the Earth offers us as the sun goes down beyond the horizon.

# Height

An essential aspect of architectural lighting design is the height at which light sources are installed. The spatial relationship between a light source, the ground plane, the ceiling plane, and our bodies determines how we understand, occupy, and explore the limits of our surroundings. At a great distance a light fixture may go unnoticed even if its visual effects are perceived, while in bodily proximity, a light fixture can become a reference point, influencing the ways in which we interact with or move about a space. In addition to these spatial effects, the height of a light source can also be used to control luminance levels or evoke new concepts and durations of time. Height is a powerful variable in architectural lighting design, capable of provoking a sense of expanded space or visual intimacy.

## The Sun: Natural Phenomena

From the sun's daily path across the sky we can observe and learn the various phenomenological possibilities and visual effects afforded through the careful consideration of height. Although approximately 93 million miles (149 million kilometers) separate the sun from the Earth, we find inexplicable comfort and a sense of intimacy in every sunrise and sunset on the horizon. Perhaps it's the compression of space between sunlight and the Earth or the assurance that twice a day the distant sun will kiss the edges of the familiar—something about the diminished height of light lends itself to feelings of comfort. The horizon, or the boundary between earth and sky or water and sky, serves as the visual datum against which the height of the sun is measured throughout the course of the day, and thus the time of day observed. In this way, the height of light is inextricably linked to our perceptions of time. Light from above recalls conditions of daylight, while light from below suggests those of dawn or dusk.

The effects of height and time in relation to light are further manifested on the surface of the

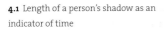

Earth in the form of shadows cast by the sun and the objects it illuminates. Throughout history, sundials—ranging in form from obelisks to time sticks to ring dials—have allowed man to scientifically track the passing of time. The temporal shadows produced by these devices are definitive measures of time as a function of height. Even without the precision afforded by a formal sundial, one can infer the time of day by the length of a shadow cast: the higher the sun, the shorter the shadows; the lower the sun, the longer the shadows. **4.1** An aerial photo of camels crossing a desert beautifully illustrates this point, as the shadows themselves become the protagonist of the image and measure the precise time at which the image was taken. **4.2**

**4.2** A herd of camels crosses Arabia's Empty Quarter, their form revealed by shadows cast by the sun.

# Intimacy

The scientific and phenomenological lessons drawn from our observations of the sun can be applied to architectural lighting design to create spaces that people immediately relate to and understand on a primitive level. Every space that we inhabit has a datum equivalent to the horizon against which we can measure the height of a light source. Often this datum is the floor of a space, while at other times it is perhaps a working surface, a dining table, or a line of furnishings against a wall. Regardless of where we find our horizons, the one constant is that our horizons are linked to our vision and thus to the physical presence of our bodies within a space. We inherently perceive the height of a light source in relationship to its closeness to our body. Just as we find visual comfort in the diminishing height of the sun relative to the horizon, we can also find comfort in the physical proximity of artificial light as it nears our bodies. A candle held in one's hand becomes a physical extension of one's body; the light it casts is a deeply personal experience, enveloping its holder in a curtain of light that renders the immediate space visible. Likewise, a desk lamp perched close to a working surface casts an area of light also appropriate for individual use, although its detachment from the individual's body infers a lesser degree of intimacy.

The relationship between intimacy and a light source's distance from the human body can be illustrated with a cross-sectional drawing through the confines of a domestic space and its adjacent public space. 4.3 Inside the most private spaces of the house (the bedroom, the study, the wardrobe, and so on) the height of a light source is kept at arm's length, as if to reinforce our eminent control and possession of this light as a means of reassurance. In more family-oriented spaces, such as the dining room, we might find a chandelier suspended over the dinner table at a distance sufficiently removed from the action below, but at the same time close

**INTIMATE**   **PERSONAL**   **SEMI-PRIVATE**   **PUBLIC (LOCAL)**   **PUBLIC (GENERAL)**

PRIVATE   PUBLIC

**4.3** Height of light relative to degree of intimacy

enough to encompass its subjects in a blanket of soft light. At the entrance of the house, the doorway is marked by a light shining from above. This luminaire—marking the boundary between exterior and interior, public and private—has dual functions, as it can be considered both the highest of private lights and the lowest of public lights. Ultimately, the streetlights and sidewalk lampposts at the end of the driveway dwarf the entrance light and those within the house, marking the shift from residential to public scale. This example of the hierarchies of height found within a typical house/street sectional relationship can serve as a model for spaces of both larger and smaller architectural scales. As we humans are inclined to adjust the height of a light source to correspond to a desired level of intimacy, we can create different readings of public and private space through the variation of light height.

## Sense of Time

The careful consideration of height in lighting design affords one the opportunity to manipulate the daily cycle of light and introduce new sensations and durations of time within a given space. As previously discussed, we are accustomed to watching the sun rise and fall over the course of its daily journey through the sky, a cycle that reinforces a very specific

**4.4 and 4.5** Downlight condition for daytime use (top) and uplight
condition for nighttime use (bottom)

**opposite**

Leslie Gill (architect) and L'Observatoire International (lighting design), Edison School Distance Learning Centers lighting mock-up, 2002: This project aims to illuminate a classroom environment where both human and virtual instruction take place. The directionality of the light can imply the time of day (downlight condition for daytime, uplight for nighttime) or the mode of instruction (downlight for typical classroom-style instruction, uplight for virtual instruction to minimize computer-screen glare).

**4.6** Varying conditions are created with light height, signaling time and intimacy: High-output downlights and three raised pendant fixtures illuminated for daytime conditions (left), two raised and one lowered pendant fixture illuminated for day to evening transition (middle), and medium-output uplights and single low pendant fixture over dining table illuminated for nighttime condition (right).

sense of passing time. In architectural interiors, the control of this daylight or the introduction of new man-made cycles of light can influence the speed, the emotion, and the use of a space. For example, by day, one might specify the use of ceiling cove lighting to graze the face of a wall, while by night, these lights can be replaced by floor-mounted uplights that illuminate this same wall from below. While the architecture remains the same, one's perception of the space is dramatically altered through the implied height and the control of the lighting. 4.4 and 4.5 During the day, the light from above draws one's eye to the upper limits of the space, and the extent of its scale is revealed. At night, the light from below surrounds the visitor like an all-encompassing cocoon; the visual extent of the space is confined to the realm illuminated by the glow of light at the base of the wall. These two lighting conditions can also be utilized over a more compressed period of time in order to give purpose to a given event, such as a dining experience. Other manipulations of lighting height that can similarly affect one's perception of time include the mechanical lowering of pendant fixtures over a dining table or the incremental lowering of fixture height along a spatial trajectory, experienced in sequence throughout the course of the night. 4.6

# Function and Dispersement

**4.7** Width of beam spread relative to height

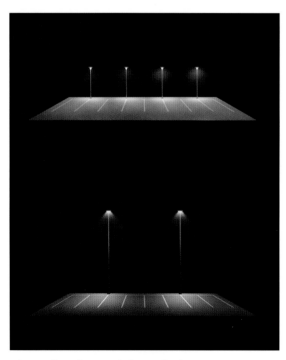

**4.8** Ground area illuminated relative to height

The height of a lighting fixture is one of several variables that affect the intensity, spread, and perceived brightness of a given light source. Two light sources with identical illumination and beam spreads will be able to illuminate different areas, depending on the height at which they are installed. As height increases, so does the diameter of the conic beam of light, and thus light of increased height can generally illuminate a greater surface area. 4.7 Likewise, a single high light source or several lower light sources can illuminate an equal area. In this case, the quantity of light becomes a function of both the height and density of light fixtures installed. 4.8

The visual principle of height is also essential in ensuring the functionality of a space. Task lighting—lighting that enables the successful performance of a given activity—demands the proximity of a light source to the anticipated task. Ultimately it is up to the lighting designer to determine what visual, programmatic, and spatial effect he or she wishes to achieve in order to designate an appropriate height for the luminaires in question. The following summations can help clarify the varied effects of function and distribution in relation to the height of a light source:

A single luminaire installed at great height will cast a single beam of light that exhibits the following qualities:
—The area illuminated will be a function of height: the higher the fixture, the larger the area illuminated.
—The luminaire will become the focal point of a space, as our eyes are drawn to the brightest spot around.
—The light emitted by the luminaire will blanket the surroundings in an unequivocally even glow, eliminating all sense of hierarchy or patches of darkness within the space.

Multiple luminaires installed at lower heights will cast multiple beams of light that exhibit the following qualities:

—The area illuminated will be a function of height and density: several low-height luminaires can illuminate a comparable area to that of a high-height luminaire.

—No single luminaire will become the focal point of the space. Rather, one's eyes will shift around the space to the various areas of brightness.

—The light emitted by the luminaires will overlap or remain separate to create areas of greater or lesser brightness. Variety in lighting effect and hierarchy is perceived.

The decision to use a single high light source versus multiple lower light sources is one that must take into account desired function and experience. A single light source of great height can often feel imposing, leaving visitors with the uncomfortable sensation of literally being in the spotlight. However, such a light source can also have great power when used in an appropriate context, such as that of a church, a stage set, or a place where a heightened sense of drama is desired. L'Observatoire International often employs several light sources at lower heights in order to introduce variety in brightness and contrast, and thus a varied experience within a space. An example of such a condition is the installation of a lighting canopy over an exterior public space or plaza in lieu of the placement of several single light sources of greater height along the perimeter. 4.9 The distributed lighting ensures the proper illumination of the space and the decreased height creates a kind of enclosure or permeable ceiling to the plaza. Beneath such a canopy of light, a visitor feels secure knowing that the magic and comfort of this light is almost literally within reach.

**4.9** Polshek Partnership Architects, RW2 (interior design), and L'Observatoire International (lighting design), The Standard Hotel, New York, New York, 2009: A lighting canopy over an exterior lounge space creates an intimate and sheltered environment.

# Density

In contrast to the vast spatial extremes made possible by the variable of height, density—measured in feet or meters—controls the movement and rhythm of a space through quantity and spatial composition of light sources. Like the percussion section of an orchestra, the density of light in tandem with existing architectural patterns can establish the tempo of a space, giving a rhythm and movement to the overall architectural composition. 5.1 The intersection and overlays of architectural and luminary patterns can create unexpected counterpoints, syncopations of form and light that guide a visitor.

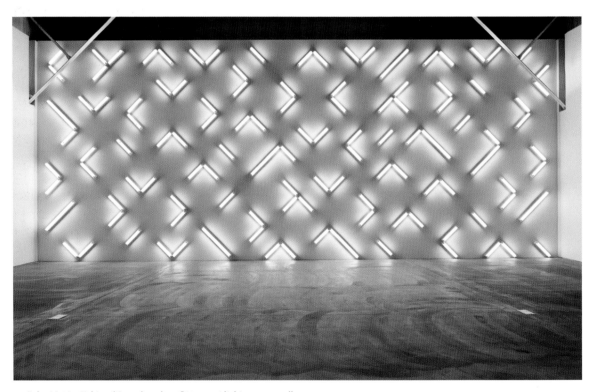

**5.1** Robert Irwin, *Light and Space* (2007), 115 fluorescent lights on one wall

# Parameters

The visual principle of density can be defined by two parameters: the number of fixtures in a given area and the organizational character of a grouping of fixtures. Together, the careful control of both quantitative and organizational variables permits lighting designers a great range of opportunity in their quest to light a space. While certain standards of density do exist for particular spaces or programs (one such standard could be the designated installation of lampposts at approximately three meter, or ten foot, intervals in an urban thoroughfare), there is truly no definitive formula that can be implemented to suit all conditions. Density, like the other five visual principles of light, has components of both quantifiable science and subjective judgment, and ultimately, our visual understanding of the effects of densities in a given space can vary by project, program, or emotion.

While the objective measure of density (the first parameter) serves to establish the spacing and rhythms of light through precise numeric count, what we truly perceive when immersed in a space is the magnitude of one density relative to another. L'Observatoire International often employs the juxtaposition of two or more different density types to convey hierarchies and spatial relationships within a given space. In addition to the relative magnitude of density, the organizational character of fixture placement (the second parameter) is also a subjective factor that eludes scientific precision. However, for pedagogical clarity we will categorize organizational character into three typologies—linear, random, and organized pattern. Linear organization refers to a lighting condition where the effect of a grouping of fixtures is perceived as a single, linear light. This most often occurs when individual fixtures are concealed within a recessed cove, creating the illusion of a continuous source of light where the visual effect of a single fixture is indistinguishable from that of the group. Random organization

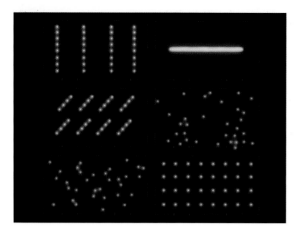

**5.2** Space can be organized through varied light densities and patterns.

describes a grouping of light fixtures whose individual placement follows no geometric logic and whose holistic organization thus defies a specific pattern. In contrast, the individual placement of lights in an organized pattern follows geometric logic, and their holistic organization can be categorized as a recognizable shape or pattern. Such a pattern most often takes the form of a line or a grid. Together with the numeric count, these organizational patterns help determine the ways in which we perceive and choose to implement varying densities of light in design. 5.2

## Hierarchy and Power

Our contemporary understanding of artificial light as an egalitarian commodity to which we have equal access deviates from the historic implications of artificial light. It was not so long ago that the liberal use and display of artificial light was an expensive luxury available only to the well-to-do, and thus a visual indicator and symbol of status and wealth. People of lesser means rationed their use of candles at night, lighting only the minimum number required for a task, while those of greater wealth could afford to be more liberal in their use of candles and light. The commonly used phrase "early to bed, early to rise" embodies the notion that one was encouraged to be resourceful of natural daylight and sparing of candlelight.[1]

Contraptions that hold concentrated displays of light, such as a chandelier, were coveted objects that if held in a household collection were most often placed in prominent domestic spaces as centerpieces for entertainment. Large concentrations of exterior lights were used to demarcate places of great importance, and flames or lamps kept burning through the course of the night were true luxuries permitted only to the wealthy. As candles were replaced in the early part of the nineteenth century by brighter and more efficient lamps that burned oil, petroleum,

5.3 View of buildings in Singapore by night

or kerosene, the economic implications and status associated with the liberal use of man-made light remained unchanged. It was only with Thomas Edison's invention of the electric filament and the subsequent proliferation of electricity that electric lighting became commonplace, no longer a luxury but a domestic necessity.

Today, the cost of man-made light in the developed world has diminished since the days of candles, and access to a light switch or to power is most often taken for granted. By night, the average city is a spectacle of twinkling lights demarcating the windows of empty office buildings, and the typical household's lights often remain on even when its occupants are elsewhere. 5.3 However, we only need to look to a satellite image of our world at night to regain an understanding of the implicit power symbolized through densities of artificial light. 5.4 In this map, the regions of greatest development and economic influence are those with the highest densities of light. Like constel-

**5.4** The city lights of Earth

lations of stars in the vast Milky Way, we can read in this map the figurative stories of our global history and visualize the economic power of America, Europe, China, and Japan, the connectivity of the Trans-Siberian Railway, the insistent production of oil in the Middle East, or the resultant coastal inhabitation of postcolonial South America. While in our daily lives it is easy to forget the symbolic power associated with densities of light, clearly, on a greater scale, these implications still exist.

In lighting design, we can apply the concept of power in density to give hierarchy and order to a space. Like a city skyline, whose monumental buildings command the viewer's attention through the liberal use of light by night, an architectural space can be lit with differing densities of lighting that signify to the visitor places of greater and lesser importance. For example, in lighting the exterior of a building it is common to use a greater density of light sources

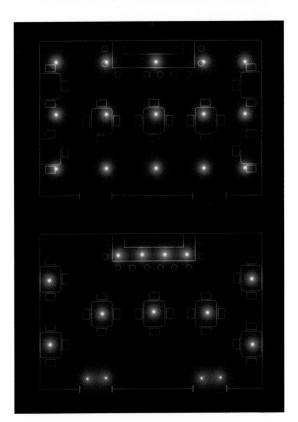

**5.5** Densities of light in space: Evenly spaced lighting irrespective of program (top) and lighting organized with regard to program (bottom)

## Rhythm and Movement

at principal entrances and gathering spaces. While the visual effect of density is invariably linked to the other five visual principles (e.g., one can achieve the same light levels with a single light source of greater illuminance as with multiple light sources of lesser illuminance), multiple light sources used together still command a sense of power and importance like that of the seventeenth-century chandelier or the concentrations of light on the satellite map. Similarly, in interior spaces the installation of light sources in groups of varying density can alter the way we perceive and move through a space. The same quantity of light fixtures rearranged in different permutations of densities within a room can drastically alter one's understanding of programmatic hierarchies. 5.5

Beyond the fundamentals of providing adequate vision, urban lighting can also serve as an organizer and a conveyer of spatial hierarchies while giving a visual identity to a city. Densities of light fixtures are essential in providing a visual reading of the hierarchy of varied passageways and public spaces. While city laws often mandate different illuminance levels for the circulation of vehicles and pedestrians based on street traffic speed and frequency of use, the density of fixtures can further aid in achieving these varied intensities while visually conveying a street's relative importance. In such a way, the visual property of density can be an essential component in determining the hierarchy of infrastructural elements in an overall urban composition. 5.6

The familiar analogy that music and architecture share much in common is perhaps most prevalent in their common ability to choreograph sequential progressions through time and space. These sequences are governed by repetitive patterns of dissonant schemes that influence behaviors and movements over time, thus giving lyrical shape to a holistic composition. In architecture, such patterns are embodied

**5.6** Aerial photograph of Paris, France: Light densities signal infrastructural hierarchies and urban organization.

by the concept of rhythm, realized through the presence of proportional relationships and the implementation of repeating forms and spatial schemes. The desire to bring a cohesive order to architecture through the use of rhythmic repetitions can be traced back to the time of the ancient Greeks, when buildings were designed in accordance to rational, proportional systems believed to represent the harmony of the universe, similar to those that governed the realm of music. The use of proportional systems and rhythmic elements has prevailed throughout the history of architecture, appearing and reappearing in the treatises of milestone movements from the Romans to the Renaissance to modernism.

**5.7** Star clusters in the night sky create legible forms and densities.

As with music or audio input, our cognitive capacities respond well to patterns and are more easily confused by unrelated elements strung together without pattern or sequence. (It is for this reason that we are more apt to memorize sequences of words in poetry that follow the structure of repetition and verse than those in prose alone.) Lighting is one of many elements within a greater architectural composition that can be used repetitively or in sequence in order to organize a space. Just as columns, beams, windows, and other forms or materials can be implemented as repeating units, lighting too can create rhythms that play in tandem with those of its surroundings.

Differing rhythmic densities of light have the capacity to link or fracture spaces in sequence. An abrupt change in density will solicit a jump or pause, while the continuity of related densities will encourage uniform movement and experience. Furthermore, densities of light can create a sense of either monotony or playfulness within a space. The redundant use of one fixture type or lighting condition can easily provoke boredom, but a variation of densities can enliven an otherwise mundane space. We only need to look to the night sky and our Milky Way to be reminded that density variations are visually interesting. In the clusters of stars, we discover shapes and symbols, stories and myths that fuel the imagination. 5.7

## Narrative

Such a narrative approach to lighting densities inspired the logic behind the architecture and light installation the Pink Project (2008), sponsored by the Make it Right Foundation in commemoration of Hurricane Katrina. On this occasion, L'Observatoire International was invited to light a temporary installation by Los Angeles–based architects Graft, built for the inaugural fundraising event for the Lower Ninth Ward in New Orleans. The installation—composed of hundreds of temporary structures clad in

**this page**

Graft (architect) and L'Observatoire International (lighting design), the Pink Project, Make it Right Foundation, New Orleans, Louisiana, 2008

**5.8** Installation for the foundation's inaugural event, fundraising for the Lower Ninth Ward reconstruction

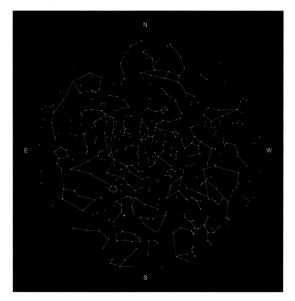

**5.9** Star constellations on August 26, 2005—the day that Hurricane Katrina made landfall in New Orleans

pink and spread over the equivalent area of fourteen city blocks—aimed to represent the renewal and reordering of the neighborhood, which was devastated by the 2005 hurricane. L'Observatoire International's conceptual approach to the lighting of this installation was to overlay two light densities symbolic of two very different stories: one of the future and one of the past. The pink structures themselves were lit from within, conjuring an orderly vision of the reconstruction of future neighborhoods. 5.8 A secondary system of lighting, in the form of thousands of tiny points of light, was deployed in clusters that recalled the cosmic positioning of the stars on the eve of Hurricane Katrina, and in quantities that symbolized the number of people who disappeared in the events of the hurricane. 5.9 and 5.10 By creating these two legible densities of light, the site became imbued with an important narrative, one that spoke of both history and the future promise of this place. Light densities such as the ones in the Pink Project have the capacity of conveying stories and ideas that add layers of symbolic meaning, fueling novel interpretations of architectural projects.

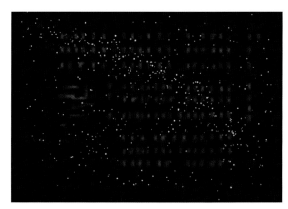

**5.10** Plan of lighting concept for week six of the Pink Project's site installation: Superimposition of two symbolic light densities

# Space Navigation and Depth Perception

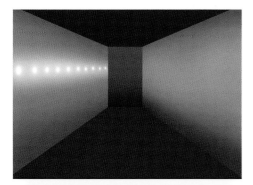

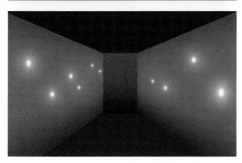

**5.11** Varied densities of light in a corridor affect perception of depth.

The numeric density of lighting fixtures, along with their organizational characteristics, plays an important role in controlling the manner in which we perceive and navigate through space. Changes in density have the power to quicken the tempo and heighten the energy of a space, or, alternatively, slow down the pace or evoke a sense of stasis. The spatial organization of fixtures into different patterns of density can further augment or negate the ways in which numeric densities affect our perception of time and depth. For example, ten fixtures in a given passageway can create vastly different effects when organized in different patterns. If the fixtures are placed at approximately one meter (three feet) on center at the same height along the span of one wall, they will visually emphasize the length of the corridor and the diminishment of the single-point perspective. If the fixtures are placed one meter on center but in an alternating sequence on both walls, the staggered effect breaks the exaggerated visual reading of a diminished perspective, and the corridor therefore appears shorter. If the ten fixtures are placed at random throughout the length of the corridor, the perspectival tunnel effect is almost completely broken, and the nonpattern formed by the random constellation of lights dominates the visual field. 5.11 Through thoughtful use and control of light density patterns, one has the ability to influence the ways in which visitors move through and interact with a given space and, as in the case of the corridor, visually alter the perspectival reading and perceived depth of architectural space.

1    Marshall B. Davidson, "Early American Lighting," *The Metropolitan Museum of Art Bulletin, New Series* 3, no. 1 (Summer 1944): 30–40.

# Direction and Distribution

If light is thought of as a malleable medium that can be directed, channeled, and molded, then the lighting designer is a sculptor who determines the form light takes in an architectural setting. He has the ability to determine the direction of light and its beam characteristics, giving it concrete or intangible form. In turn, the architecture will engage in a game of reciprocity, further sculpting the light while simultaneously being visually sculpted by the effects of light. The form of light is governed by the principle of direction and distribution, which concerns the aim, shape, and beam characteristics of a light source. A narrow beam can cut through a space to highlight a specific place, while a wide beam might illuminate a great area, expanding one's visual grasp of his or her surroundings. These are the physical dimensions and phenomenological potentials of light that the principle of direction and distribution govern.

## Permutations and Effects

The direction and distribution of light can be qualified by several concrete terms that are fundamental to the vocabulary of a lighting designer. The directionality of light is generally described in one of three directions—up, down, or multidirectional—and its resultant application on an object or area as direct or indirect. The distribution of light is generally

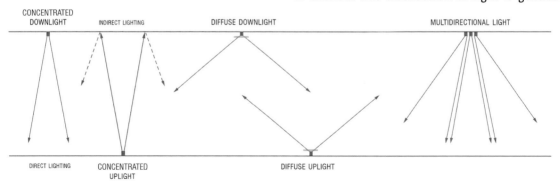

**6.1** Direction and distribution of light

6.2a

6.2b

6.2c

6.2d

6.2e

6.2f

**6.2a – 6.2f** Different direction and distribution of light within a room can create varied spatial effects.

either concentrated, where light is focused on a narrow area, or diffuse, where light is dispersed over a wide area. The pairing of differing directionalities and distributions provides a lighting designer with many possibilities for rendering an object or space to differing effect. 6.1

Take, for example, the lighting of a given room. The following seven possible permutations of direction and distribution offer up multiple lighting options, resulting in different readings of space:

—An indirect-diffuse uplight will illuminate the ceiling of the room, drawing our eyes to the upper limits of the space. The ceiling in this case may itself become a perceivable light source. 6.2a

—A direct-diffuse downlight will illuminate the floor or intermediary plane in the room, making it the prominent surface. If the floor is illuminated, it will visually ground the visitor in the space. 6.2b

—An indirect-concentrated uplight will create an area of high luminance on the ceiling. 6.2c

—A direct-concentrated downlight will create an area of high luminance on the floor and high contrasts within the space. 6.2d

—A multidirectional-concentrated light source will offer up nonuniform brightness in the space, calling the viewer's attention to specific areas highlighted in the room. 6.2e

—A multidirectional-diffuse light will evenly illuminate various surfaces in a space, minimizing contrasts and the presence of shadows. 6.2f

**6.3a and 6.3b** Directional lighting's ability to amplify or negate a material's surface texture is evident when comparing an uplight grazing (left) and a frontlight washing (right) a brick wall.

**6.4a – 6.4f** Direction and distribution of light and shadows can greatly affect the appearance of form.

In addition to its ability to visually expand or compress our perceptions of space, the direction and distribution of light has the capacity to accentuate or negate the presence of objects and form. What we perceive as three-dimensionality is simply patterns of brightness and darkness juxtaposed against one another. Direct light that grazes a surface has the power to render a material's textures, patterns, and imperfections visible through high contrast. Such an effect can be used to a lighting designer's advantage to heighten the visual reading of a material or surface. A brick wall grazed with uplighting will appear complex, dramatic, and tactile. The same brick wall illuminated with a diffuse, direct light will appear flat and even, its nooks and crannies virtually erased. 6.3a and 6.3b

In lighting objects, varied combinations of direction and distribution can yield drastically different effects. Concentrated light can be utilized to provoke a sense of drama and visual excitement in the appearance of the object it illuminates. However, the sharp shadows cast by such a light source may be detrimental to the reading of details, as portions of the object are invariably disguised by darkness. An even, diffuse light is better suited to equally render all parts of the piece visible, but the mood induced by this type of lighting is often static and bland.

The directionality of lighting can also dramatically transform one's perception of an object in space, sculpting it to stand out or meld into its surrounding environment. A concentrated downlight will emphasize an object's form and texture while casting dramatic shadows that often evoke an eerie sense of the uncanny. A concentrated uplight will also emphasize an object's plasticity of form, but the shadows produced are often strange and unfamiliar. A sidelight can effectively enhance one's reading of shape and form in a natural manner reminiscent of sunlight. A frontlight will flatten the reading of an object, rendering all visible form in equal light. A backlight will render the object in silhouette, placing emphasis on its holistic form. 6.4a – 6.4f Through the direction of light, one can alter the visual structure of a composition in space, guiding the eye to places of heightened contrast and revealing unexpected tensions between flatness and depth, foreground and background, object and architecture.

## Forms of Light and their Potential in Transforming Space

The careful control of distribution and directionality of light is a lighting designer's most powerful tool in defining and revealing the limits of space. For example, diffuse lighting can be utilized to create shifting atmospheres and mystical backdrops, while directional light can create the illusion of stasis, of a concrete place revealed at a precise time. One can look to the transient magic of light in a stage production for visual cues that can be effectively applied to the realm of architectural lighting. Perhaps one of the most intriguing aspects of stage lighting design is its ability to transform a small space and transport its viewer into a multitude of imaginary worlds over a short period of time. Here, the varied direction and distribution of light are crucial to the ongoing transformation, as margins and borders of architectural bodies seemingly appear and disappear, divide and unify, guiding a continuum or break of motion through time and space.

In the stage productions of Robert Wilson, lighting effects often substitute for backdrops or other representations of architecture, and it is precisely the sculpting of this light that gives rise to the novel spaces on stage. A strip of light projected onto an elevation or floor can act as a powerful incision, slicing a space into two separate worlds. 6.5 A concentrated beam of light can completely envelope an actor's physical and mental being, transporting him into an alternate realm. A projected rectangle of light may be perceived as an aperture or doorway that

6.5

transports the character and audience into another world. 6.6a – 6.6c The alternative narrative presented through light in stage lighting design runs parallel to that of the spoken word, but operates on its own terms and in its own time. The lighting narrative diverges when necessary, transforming spaces and manipulating durations of time. Likewise in architecture, the form and directionality of light is a story to be experienced simultaneously with that of built form, but it can also add a secondary layer of experience.

Light can formally accentuate lines, planes, and seams in architecture or, alternatively, diverge from the logic of built structure and introduce its own language of form and space. As in theatrical stage design, a sharp beam of light can be used to divide space, creating a visual threshold, or a cone

of light can carve an alternate space within the confines of the greater whole. Such effects are present in L'Observatoire International's lighting of the Guthrie Theater in Minneapolis, Minnesota (2006), by Ateliers Jean Nouvel. In this project, the literal theatricality of program drives the concept of the lighting, and its directionality and distribution take on dramatic effects. This aesthetic trajectory is established from the very moment one approaches the theater: from the exterior, one's first encounter with the building is marked by a concentrated beam of light cast onto the entrance pavement, visually demarcating a threshold between the everyday world and the theatrical realm about to be entered (see figure 12.4 on page 116). Within the building the theatrical experience continues to unfold, as realized through stagelike lighting effects (further described on pages 114–19).

Consideration of alternate spaces made possible through the control of light direction and distribution is not limited to the realm of theater. These spaces can be implemented in many other architectural environments, such as restaurants and retail shops, redefining the relationship between built and experienced space. In restaurants it is often effective to downlight each table with a concentrated beam in order to create individual spaces for the diners, defined by the narrow confines of this light. Likewise, narrow-beam accent lights can be used in retail shops to spotlight objects of great importance, making them glow at the center of their own universe.

**6.5 (opposite) and 6.6a – 6.6c** Scenes from Robert Wilson's production *Pelléas et Mélisande*—held in Salzburg, Austria, in 1997—show the use of projected light forms in evoking and organizing theatrical space.

# Architecture as Lantern

Thus far we have discussed the formal qualities of light made possible by application. However, the concept of direction and distribution is one that is truly independent from the latest technologies, and that existed long before the advent of electricity. The desire to sculpt light into shapes and patterns, imbued with function and meaning, is a timeless phenomenon that finds its roots in man's most primitive constructions. Throughout the history of architecture, there are endless examples where light form and built form are virtually inextricable from one another. Historically, daylight was viewed as a powerful and ever-changing resource that could be harnessed for spiritual purposes through man-made construction. In order to control and give form to transient daylight, it was often channeled through a substance or medium. The resultant light thus became a sort of synthetic memory of the material or form through which it passed—a new, distinct element in space with its own formal properties and effects, reminiscent of its parent architecture.

Ancient earthworks and primitive constructions provide exceptional examples of the ways that natural light can be channeled into novel form to produce unexpected effects. For example, the ruins of Chaco Canyon, Arizona—a major center of Anasazi Indian culture between 850 and 1250 CE—demonstrate a definitive understanding of the cycles of natural light and the desire to harness this resource for spiritual and practical purposes. The sites in Chaco Canyon were constructed in sync with the ritual of the sun and channeled sunlight into figural beams, lines, and rectangles that marked the calendar cycle and the passing of time. Furthermore, the solar orientation of the building sites and the positioning of windows close to grade channeled the direct warmth and light of the low winter sun while blocking the direct, burning rays of the high summer sun. Through architecture the Anasazi established a seasonal control of direct and diffuse light in their living

**6.7** Pueblo Bonito ruins, Chaco Canyon, Arizona

and ceremonial spaces, making light both a figural and practical element. 6.7

Another wonderful example of light channeled by architecture to serve a specific purpose emerges from the oculus of the Pantheon of Rome (118–28 CE). This building sculpts light into a powerful, independent form evocative of the divine spirituality it aimed to embody. Through the course of the day, a projected circle of light emerges from the oculus and sweeps the circumference of the dome. The dominant directionality of the light (from above) and its concentrated effect transform the interior into a mysterious space of great atmospheric extremes. The channeled light calls attention to itself and the space it illuminates, while much of the rest of the Pantheon's interior remains enshrouded in secretive shadows. 6.8

In these two examples, the opacity and weight of a building structure dictate the limits of how light is permitted to enter a space. It can be argued that the need to increase light levels in buildings and the desire to create new sensations and forms of light drove many of the historic inventions in architectural structure. During the Gothic period, pointed and ribbed vaulting systems were developed to support more weight, thus opening up more space to windows. Flying buttresses enabled the transfer of forces to be carried to an exterior skeleton, making large expanses of stained glass on the periphery walls feasible. A few hundred years later, the Enlightenment period cultivated a fascination with the didactic of light and dark, clear and obscure, good and evil, and light's ability to provoke the phenomenological sensations of the sublime influenced the form of architecture, its admittance of light, and its production of dark space. French architect Étienne-Louis Boullée, who called himself an inventor of the "architecture of shadows," sought to give tangible shape to darkness (and light) with the aid of simple architectural geometries.[1] His proposal

**6.8** The oculus of the Pantheon of Rome, Italy

**6.9** Cross section through Étienne-Louis Boullée's Cenotaph for Newton project (1783)

for a Cenotaph for Newton (1783), a spherical building whose planetarium-like interior aimed to evoke the experience of the star-filled heavens, was in its essence a container for darkness punctuated by light. Here, darkness was sculpted into the legible form of a sphere, and light into pinpoint-like stars. 6.9

Ultimately, the desire to eradicate the mysteries of shadows, and to render all things equally visible through light, propelled architecture into an age of transparency, precision, and equality, rendered through evenly distributed light. The conceptual shift in the historic understanding of light as revealer versus eradicator of mystery was also accompanied by a change of form. In the nineteenth century—the great age of iron and glass—light admitted into a transparent envelope was dispersed through intricately woven surfaces of glass and sparkling metal, taking the form of a sort of membranous construct, a diffuse cocoon that enveloped space. No longer was light to be conceived as an independent element channeled through architecture, but light and architecture became one and the same. The twentieth-century glass skyscraper epitomized the notion that the skin of a building could literally be constructed from light, as the light-admitting envelope truly became an element of its own, divorced from its formal, load-bearing structure. This new kind of multidirectional, evenly distributed light supported emerging notions of spatial democracy gaining momentum in the workforce. Light admitted through the transparent envelope of an office building or factory erased the spatial and programmatic hierarchies that had previously been organized around incoming pockets of isolated light.[2]

These and other examples of controlled daylight demonstrate the many directions and distributions of light that form and materiality of architecture can dictate. However, running in parallel to this historic reading of the evolution of natural lighting with respect to architectural form is the equally relevant story of artificial light and the advancement of its genre. While candle power directed and distributed light in architectural settings for thousands of years, the advent of electricity marked a turning point in the history of artificial light and its relationship to architecture. Unlike daylight, whose presence is undeniably linked to building envelope and time of day, man-made means enable light to operate both together and independent of apertures and time, redefining the ways in which spaces are experienced. Electric lighting in particular has allowed designers to further explore the spatial potential of varied directions and distributions that complement or contrast, amplify or negate, the desired effects of natural light, animating architecture in new ways. Some of these varied effects are discussed in the first section of this chapter, but because electric light is still relatively in its infancy—having only been at our disposal for a little more than one hundred years—more applications will surely emerge in time. Technology will continue to facilitate design intentions, giving unequivocal precision to a light beam's properties, but since light waves will always be revealed through the materials they encounter, the spatial effects perceived will always be dependent on built form.

This inherent symbiosis of light and architecture is what inspires the work of L'Observatoire International today. While architectural projects vary in form and design intent, and the subsequent lighting employed responds accordingly, the ideal relationship between light and architecture is one of mutual enhancement. Thus, the most successful collaborations between lighting designer and architect are those where integration of light and built form is totally seamless; in this sense, the architecture almost becomes porous to light, and the two become one and the same. In order to achieve such ideal assimilation, a lighting designer must approach a project with design empathy, and an architect must trust the lighting designer not as a subcontractor, but as a true collaborator, so that their ultimate goals and vision of space are shared.

Because a lighting designer is often invited to collaborate on a project at a secondary stage—when an architect's vision of form, structure, and experience is in place—the challenge is to integrate light in such a way that its very presence is inherent to the original architectural intentions. A skilled lighting designer can successfully work with an existing material and formal palette, transforming architecture into a metaphorical lantern for light, and light into a medium that reveals and enhances the architect's visions of formal space. Ultimately, the best lighting in architecture simply evokes an atmosphere, an emotion, a memory of a space in time inextricable from the architecture's very being.

1 Isabelle Hyman and Marvin Trachtenberg, *Architecture: From Prehistory to Post-modernism* (New York: Harry N. Abrams, 1986), 421–23.

2 For further reading on the late-nineteenth-century emergence of the notion of an egalitarian light in the working environment, see Henry Plummer, *Masters of Light, First Volume: Twentieth Century Pioneers* (Tokyo: a+u, 2003), 34–38, 54–56.

# Analysis

The following analyses aim to provide definitive examples of the ways in which the six visual principles of light influence and determine the experiential and practical effects of lighting design in a project. Six projects exhibiting a wide range of geographic and programmatic diversity have been selected from L'Observatoire International's portfolio to be analyzed and diagrammed with respect to the previous section's contents. Each project analysis describes the overall lighting concept, the specified fixtures, and the methods of architectural integrations that facilitated the subsequent result. The written descriptions are accompanied by tables that chart each luminaire's approximate illuminance, luminance, color, height, density, and direction and distribution with respect to their placement in the space and in relation to one another. (These tables primarily aim to convey a luminaire's visual effects in relationship to the others employed, more so than the numerical data that facilitate such intentions.) In addition to the tables, rendered plans and sections diagram the placement and general effect of the luminaires, further illustrating the organizations and spatial hierarchies conceived through light. Finally, in order to clearly illustrate the relationship between light, its visual principles, and the resultant spatial effects, we have in some cases chosen to focus on specific spaces or trajectories of a greater project or on the luminaires of greatest importance.

# High Line

New York, New York, United States

Project Completion: 2009

Landscape Architect: James Corner Field Operations

Architect: Diller Scofidio + Renfro

Client: New York City Economic Development Corporation,
New York City Department of Parks and Recreation, and
Friends of the High Line

Built upon the elevated tracks of a defunct freight line, the High Line is a one-of-a-kind public space in the heart of New York City, a green promenade that floats approximately ten meters (thirty-three feet) above the dizzying activity and traffic of the streets below. 7.1 and 7.2 The structure, which runs along Manhattan's West Side (between 10th and 11th Avenues) from Gansevoort Street in the Meatpacking District to Thirty-Fourth Street in Midtown, is both an urban reprieve and a privileged vantage point from which one can examine the activity of the city. Along its linear yet experientially diverse trajectory, the High Line nestles itself between built structures, passes underneath existing buildings, and carves through others. The desire to call attention to these unique spatial relationships drove the concept of the lighting design employed throughout.

The overall lighting strategy of this project is twofold. First, the lighting aims to promote an unobstructed view of the city at night from the elevated tracks. By shielding light sources and keeping most luminaires below eye level, visual connection to the greater surroundings is not impeded. Second, the lighting also aims to establish a low and consistent plane of light along the length of the park, making the elevated tracks appear to float over the city below. This effect is achieved through the employment of several lighting typologies that simultaneously provide visibility, safety, and unobtrusive lighting over the length of the High Line by night.

## Walkway

The High Line's landscaped walkway is illuminated by soft perimeter lighting, installed on the underside of the guardrail structure and by low-rail walkway lights situated along the periphery of the pedestrian path. 7.3 The linear LEDs concealed along the underside of the guardrails cast a cool, soft glow on the plantings and walkways. 7.4 and 7.5 The additional low-rail LED walkway lights are installed to provide

| | LIGHT SOURCE | ILLUMINANCE | LUMINANCE | COLOR | HEIGHT | DENSITY | DIRECTION / DISTRIBUTION |
|---|---|---|---|---|---|---|---|
| WALKWAY | WALKWAY PERIMETER RAIL LIGHT: LINEAR LED | 10 LUX | LOW | WARM | 1M (4 FT 3 IN) | LINEAR | DIRECT DOWN DIFFUSE |
| | WALKWAY PATH LIGHTING: LINEAR LED | 0–50 LUX | MEDIUM | WARM | 0.3 M (1 FT) | LINEAR | DIRECT DOWN DIFFUSE |
| | UNDERSIDE OF PEEL-UP BENCH LIGHTING: LINEAR LED | 20 LUX | MEDIUM | WARM | 0.6 M (2 FT) | LINEAR | INDIRECT DOWN DIFFUSE |
| TUNNEL PASSAGES | DAYTIME TUNNEL PASSAGES: LINEAR FLUORESCENT | 500 LUX | HIGH | COOL | 8 M (26 FT) | ORGANIZED PATTERN | DIRECT DOWN DIFFUSE |
| | NIGHTTIME TUNNEL PASSAGES: LINEAR FLUORESCENT | 100 LUX | HIGH | BLUE | 8 M (26 FT) | ORGANIZED PATTERN | DIRECT DOWN DIFFUSE |
| ACCESS POINTS | ACCESS POINT POLE LIGHT: METAL HALIDE | 100 LUX | MEDIUM | COOL | 5 M (16 FT) | RANDOM (1 PER STAIRWELL) | DIRECT DOWN CONCENTRATED |
| | PUNCTUAL LANDSCAPE LIGHT: METAL HALIDE | 50 LUX | MEDIUM | WARM | 0.3 M (1 FT) | RANDOM | DIRECT UP DIFFUSE |

**7.1** High Line: Artificial light implementation table

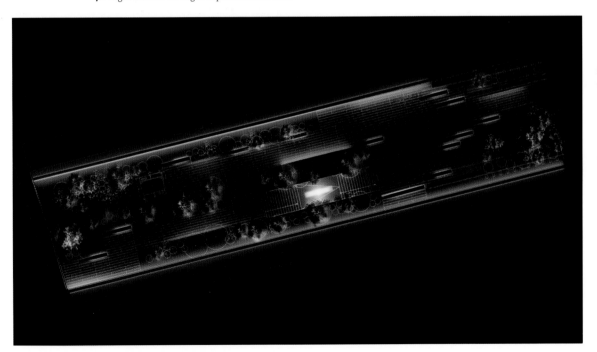

**7.2** A rendered light plan of the High Line walkway (Gansevoort Street entrance) shows the different lighting typologies deployed throughout.

**7.4 and 7.5 (opposite)** The pedestrian path and plantings are illuminated by concealed low-rail LED lights.

**7.3** A rendered light section through the High Line shows an assortment of lighting typologies.

Analysis

additional downlight directly upon the path they follow. In order to direct the pedestrian's attention toward the impressive verticality of the surroundings (the towering skyscrapers and the endless sky), both of these light sources are kept at low illuminance levels, and the height of the fixtures is maintained below chest height, even when one is seated. The concealed fixtures minimize luminance contrast and glare such that one perceives the effect of the lights, not the fixtures themselves. The cooler color temperature of the LED lighting provides a counterpoint to the incandescent glow of the surrounding buildings and to the warm light of the setting sun. By night, bathed in the cool, white light of the linear LEDs, the diverse plantings glow vibrant amber and green.

While the linear LEDs succeed in illuminating the carpet of low-rising perennials, grasses, and shrubs, a secondary lighting source is needed to light trees of a larger scale. In this case, spike-mounted, incandescent uplights are placed accordingly throughout the landscape, rendering the canopies of the trees in a soft, warm glow. The warm, white color temperature of this light differentiates these vertical plantings from the cooler carpet of light rendered below. The light sources themselves are again concealed to minimize visual distraction and glare. The resultant lit trees punctuate the length of the High Line with a secondary layer of color, texture, and light, adding syncopation to the densities and rhythms of lights in the overall scheme.

The furnishings and benches positioned throughout the High Line further elaborate the patterns of light encountered over the course of the park. In particular, the benches, which peel up from the poured concrete pathways, are lit in such a way that their repetitive presence is perceived from afar. Warm, linear LED lights—concealed on the underside of the benches and aimed toward the ground— create low pockets of light that enable the benches to visually float. In aerial views, the benches appear as intensified dashes and continuous densities of light along the length of the High Line.

## Tunnel Passages

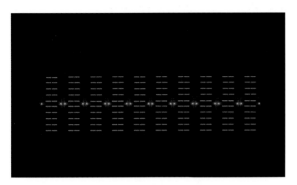

**7.6** Rendered light plan of the Chelsea Market tunnel showing use of blue fluorescent lighting by night

In the instances where the High Line passes through an existing building, the resulting tunnel-like environments acquire their own unique identity through the employment of lighting. The strategies for lighting these passages differ by day and by night. By day, a visual continuity between the open air and the covered passage is maintained through the use of cool white fluorescent tubes to illuminate the interior of the tunnels. By night, this seamless transition is broken and the tunnels are instead rendered in a deep blue light, thus acting as discernible gateways that demarcate moments of spatial transition. 7.6 – 7.8 During both day and night, the linear fluorescent tubes are visible on the walls and ceilings of the passageways, creating a rhythm of light and form reminiscent of the interiors of the industrial spaces that were once serviced by the old freight line that ran along the High Line's path.

## Access Points

**7.7** Tunnel interior at night

The various pedestrian entrances to the High Line are marked by bright white metal-halide light poles, signaling the access points at street level. These poles provide the necessary illuminance levels to allow safe ascent and descent to and from the elevated park. 7.9 and 7.10 Measuring approximately five meters (sixteen feet) in height, the poles are the highest freestanding light source installed in the landscape, and thus command the pedestrian's attention. The luminaires cast a concentrated downlight onto the staircases through the use of a precise linear lens, which ensures that this bright light is confined to the boundaries of the access points.

**7.8** View of the tunnel approach at night

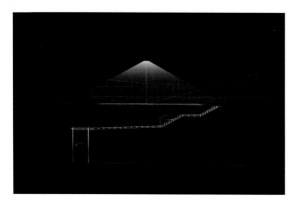

**7.9** Rendered light section through a typical access point illustrating the use of high levels of concentrated light to demarcate places of ascent to the High Line

**7.10** View from the Gansevoort Street access point up to the High Line walkway

# Newtown Creek Water Pollution Treatment Plant

Brooklyn, New York, United States

Project Completion: 2008

Architect: Polshek Partnership Architects

Engineers: Quennell Rothschild & Partners; Greeley and Hansen;
   Hazen and Sawyer; and Malcolm Pirnie

Client: New York City Department of Environmental Protection

Situated on the northern boundary of Greenpoint, Brooklyn—along the waterway that separates Brooklyn from Queens—the Newtown Creek Water Pollution Treatment Plant is a bold architectural statement of extreme city infrastructure. 8.1 – 8.3 The plant—which spans 54 acres of land and processes 230 million gallons of sewage a day, removing 85 percent of pollutants—is truly a magnificent systems network, replete with filtration, aeration, sedimentation, and digester technologies. Each of these components is formally expressed in its own architectural manner, but together they must read and operate in tandem as parts of a greater industrial machine. On a large scale, the lighting design of this project addresses how best to visually unify the plant's complex program in order to give it an identity within the wider urban composition. On a lesser scale, the lighting aims to accommodate the practical functions of the twenty-four-hour-a-day operations while visually rendering the plant as a nonthreatening, and perhaps even beautiful, entity within the context of its surrounding neighborhood.

To achieve these varied goals, the site is blanketed with a diaphanous layer of blue light that identifies the limits of the site while simultaneously visually unifying its many formal components within. 8.4 From afar, this membrane of light recalls the calm blue of water and is easily recognizable in its contrast with the constellations of orange and amber lights that otherwise define the densities and expanse of the city. From within, the soft blue blanket acts as a canvas upon which the buildings and functions can be individually distinguished through contrasting light. Circulation routes carve bright white lines in the blue, while active points such as loading docks and building entrances are rendered in warm white.

## Access Road

By night the access roads within are lit in a manner that clearly identifies the organization of circulation

| | LIGHT SOURCE | ILLUMINANCE | LUMINANCE | COLOR | HEIGHT | DENSITY | DIRECTION / DISTRIBUTION |
|---|---|---|---|---|---|---|---|
| ACCESS ROAD | STREET LIGHT: METAL HALIDE | 50 LUX | LOW | COOL | 6 M (20 FT) | 20 M (66 FT) O.C. ORGANIZED PATTERN | DIRECT DOWN DIFFUSE |
| | BOLLARD: COMPACT FLUORESCENT | 25 LUX | MEDIUM | COOL / BLUE | 1.6 M (5 FT) | 7 M (23 FT) O.C. ORGANIZED PATTERN | SIDE DIFFUSE |
| | FLOOD LIGHT ON PIPE STRUCTURE: | N/A | MEDIUM | AMBER | 1 M (3 FT) | LINEAR | DIRECT UP |
| SEDIMEN-TATION BASINS | LIGHT POLE: LINEAR FLUORESCENT | 100 LUX | MEDIUM | COOL / BLUE | 4 M (13 FT) | ORGANIZED PATTERN | MULTIDIREC. DIFFUSE |
| | ACCENT LIGHT ON POLE: METAL HALIDE | 500 LUX | HIGH | WARM | 4 M (13 FT) | ORGANIZED PATTERN | DIRECT DOWN CONCENTRATED |
| DIGESTERS | FLOOD LIGHT: METAL HALIDE | N/A | LOW | BLUE | 4 M (13 FT) OFF BASE OF DIGESTOR | ORGANIZED PATTERN / CLUSTERS OF 8 | DIRECT UP DIFFUSE |
| | WALKWAY FLOODLIGHT ALONG HORIZONTAL PASSAGE: FLUORESCENT | 150 LUX | MEDIUM | COOL | 0 M (0 FT) (FLOOR MOUNTED) | 2M (6 FT) O.C. ORGANIZED PATTERN | DIRECT UP DIFFUSE |
| | LIGHTING AT VERTICAL KNOTS ATOP DIGESTORS: LINEAR FLUORESCENT | 300 LUX | HIGH | COOL | 1.5 M (5 FT) OFF WALKWAY-FLOOR | ORGANIZED PATTERN | DIRECT SIDE CONCENTRATED |

**8.1** Newtown Creek Water Pollution Treatment Plant: Artificial light implementation table

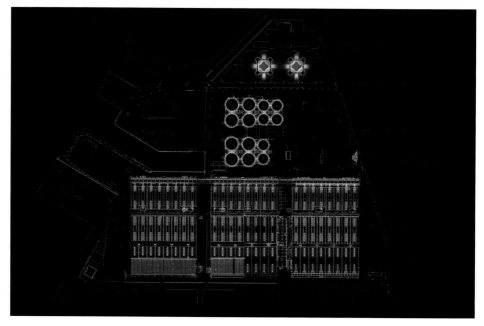

**8.2** Rendered lighting plan of the Newtown Creek Water Pollution Treatment Plant

**8.3** View of digesters illuminated with blue light

**8.4** The Newtown Creek site in relation to its urban context: A veil of blue light is used to visually unify and give identity to this large-scale infrastructural program.

in the plant while ensuring function and visibility at the level of vehicular and pedestrian traffic. The hierarchy of paths (as visible in plan through the width of a road and its breadth of light) is made possible through the implementation of a streetwide lighting system, made up of street poles and bollards. The six-meter-high (twenty-foot-tall) street poles, spaced approximately twenty meters (sixty-five feet) on center, cast a cool, white, diffuse downlight upon the surface of the roads to allow the safe navigation of vehicles. At the pedestrian scale, compact-fluorescent bollards measuring 1.6 meters (5 feet) in height are employed at a density of approximately 7 meters (23 feet) on center. The higher density of the bollards and their reduced height generates a narrower field of light that further illuminates the street

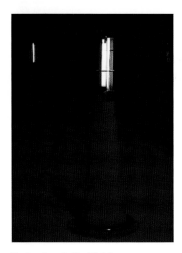

**8.5** Roadway bollard lighting simultaneously emits blue light to illuminate the landscape and white light to illuminate the roadway.

and walkways of primary roads. These bollards are designed to simultaneously emit sidelights of two different colors: the light facing the street is colored cool white, while the light facing the sidewalk is blue. 8.5 This duality helps distinguish primary circulation (white) from secondary circulation and landscape (blue) while ensuring the proper illuminance of both street and sidewalk.

Along the length of the primary access road, a monumental pipe structure servicing the sedimentation basins is uplit with warm amber light. 8.6 In turn, the buildings and loading docks serviced by the circulation are downlit with cool metal-halide or fluorescent white light. These applications of additional light along the length of the access roads provide necessary illuminance to programmatically specific places while visually articulating their presence in the overall spatial composition.

**8.6** The pipe structure servicing the sedimentation basins is lit with warm amber light. Light poles installed in the sedimentation basin area illuminate the landscape with blue light and the task area with white light. Accent lights affixed to the end of the pole's fluorescent tubes provide additional task lighting.

# Main Dining Room

**9.3** View through entrance corridor toward reception area: The corridor is illuminated by light sconces concealed behind mesh curtain walls.

The main dining room is organized around a central core composed of a bar and service area, from which the three dining spaces radiate outwards. A series of counter spaces and bar surfaces wrap around the core, providing a horizon line and visual backdrop to the dining areas. In order to visually unify this fragmented element and imply a continuity of circulation along its perimeter, the bar-height wall is illuminated with glowing, linear LED lights of an intense blue color. 9.4 Throughout the course of the night, this blue transforms into a deep amber color, signaling the passing of time. Because the furniture pieces are custom-designed to evoke the spindly structure of the Eiffel Tower, the backlight calls attention to the intricacies of their weavelike patterns and boldness of form. The contrast between the glowing wall and the silhouettes of objects and people before it adds a graphic element and drama to the space.

**9.4** A lounge and bar are surrounded by a glowing blue service counter.

**9.5** A dining table is illuminated by a custom ceiling chandelier containing both LED and low-voltage halogen lights embedded within.

The dominant light source in the main dining area is a custom chandelier system, which draws lines of structural light on the ceiling and the surrounding glass window planes that the light is reflected upon. The concept of the seemingly random-looking chandelier arose from the need to have light in the areas of the dining room where tables were not fixed. In order to accommodate the rearrangement of tables, a light source was needed that could evenly illuminate a greater area and whose formal logic was independent of any singular table arrangement. 9.5 The shape of the chandelier derives from the intricate weave of the structural elements of the Eiffel Tower, a motif that also inspired the design of plates, forks, and bar stools in the restaurant. Furthermore, knowing that the lit ceiling chandelier would be reflected onto the perimeter glass windows, the lines of its light were designed to correspond with the great streets and avenues of Paris visible through the window, speaking to the aesthetic of the city. 9.6 The glass planes present an alternative view of Paris, one in which the interior of the restaurant, its lighting, and its visitors reflected onto the spectacular view create their very own visual reinterpretation of the city.

The chandelier contains both LED and low-voltage halogen lights recessed within. The LEDs line the perimeter of the linear openings, giving formal structure to the light, while the low-voltage halogen lights scattered throughout provide a more diffuse glow. Both light sources are controlled by a dimmer, and the illuminance levels can be increased or reduced depending on the time of night and mood desired. The warm color temperature of the chandelier complements the glow of the city's night sky.

The fixed banquet tables on the periphery of the main dining spaces are individually illuminated by recessed low-voltage halogen lights installed in the ceiling. These concentrated downlights illuminate the tabletops, and are virtually invisible at

**9.6** In the main dining room, the specular surfaces of the periphery windows subtly superimpose the reflection of the interior over the exterior scene.

ceiling level so that their effect is perceived solely at the table level. In a sense, the medium luminance levels of these lights result from the reflected light produced by the bright white tablecloths. Like the ceiling chandelier, the banquet table lights also operate on dimmers, allowing illuminance levels to be adjusted throughout the course of the night. While the lights' primary function is to provide visibility and enhance the sensuous dining experience, they also create little pockets of private light that the diners inhabit.

# Beige

Tokyo, Japan

Project Completion: 2004
Architect: Peter Marino Architect
Client: Chanel Japan

Located on the top floor of the Chanel Building in Tokyo's fashionable Ginza district, Beige is a restaurant designed to reflect the identities of both the House of Chanel and of the French star chef Alain Ducasse, two major purveyors of French luxury. 10.1 and 10.2 The restaurant's projected image is embodied by the words *passion*, *style*, *boldness*, and *perfection*, which are used to describe its approach to both food and decor. Beige, a traditional color that evokes the materiality of leather and wood, serves as the decorative palette of choice and is employed throughout the interior of the restaurant to create an atmosphere of haute calm, a sophisticated respite from the bustle of everyday city life. The lighting design further facilitates this desired atmosphere by bringing added warmth and intimacy to the space while preserving the architecture's sleek aesthetic. In Beige, all light sources are concealed so that the subtleties and effects of light upon material and surface are truly perceived.

## Reception Area

Upon exiting the elevator at the tenth floor, one is welcomed into the restaurant reception area, a softly lit, corridorlike space that leads to the lounge. 10.3 Ceiling coves run the length of the walls, lit with both fluorescent and linear-incandescent lights that illuminate the subtle textures of the wall's wood panels. The height of this light (whose source is disguised within the ceiling cove) creates the illusion that light and space expand beyond the limits of the architecture. Further emphasizing the linearity of this reception area and its axial orientation toward the lounge and dining rooms is a line of bright, warm light that carves through the wooden wall, illuminating the restaurant's signage. The accessible height of this light source lends an air of intimacy and approachability to the otherwise-tall space. Diffuse steplights of low illuminance subtly guide the visitor from the reception area into the adjacent lounge.

| | LIGHT SOURCE | ILLUMINANCE | LUMINANCE | COLOR | HEIGHT | DENSITY | DIRECTION / DISTRIBUTION |
|---|---|---|---|---|---|---|---|
| **RECEPTION AREA** | CEILING COVE: XENON AND FLUORESCENT | 0–50 LUX | MEDIUM | VERY WARM | 3.5 M (11 FT) (CEILING RECESSED) | LINEAR | INDIRECT |
| | LINE ON WALL / SIGNAGE: XENON | 0–20 LUX | LOW | VERY WARM | 1 M (3 FT) (WALL RECESSED) | LINEAR | INDIRECT |
| | STEP LIGHTS: LINEAR INCANDESCENT | 20 LUX | LOW | VERY WARM | 0 M (0 FT) (FLOOR RECESSED) | LINEAR | INDIRECT |
| **LOUNGE** | TABLE ACCENT LIGHT: LOW-VOLTAGE HALOGEN | 0–70 LUX | MEDIUM | WARM | 4.5 M (13 FT 6 IN) (CEILING RECESSED) | ORGANIZED PATTERN (1 PER TABLE) | DIRECT DOWN NARROW BEAM |
| | DAYTIME WALL-WASHING DOWNLIGHT: INCANDESCENT | 0–50 LUX | MEDIUM | WARM | 4.5 M (13 FT 6 IN) (CEILING RECESSED) | 2.3 M (7 FT 6 IN) O.C. | INDIRECT DOWN |
| | NIGHTTIME WALL-WASHING UPLIGHT: XENON | 0–40 LUX | LOW | VERY WARM | 0 M (0 FT) (FLOOR RECESSED) | LINEAR | INDIRECT UPLIGHT |
| **DINING ROOM** | TABLE ACCENT LIGHT: LOW-VOLTAGE HALOGEN | 150 LUX | MEDIUM | WARM | 5 M (16 FT) (CEILING RECESSED) | ORGANIZED PATTERN (1 PER TABLE) | DIRECT DOWN NARROW BEAM |
| | GRAPHIC PATTERN / RECESSED CEILING COVE: LINEAR INCANDESCENT | 0–20 LUX | LOW | VERY WARM | 5 M (16 FT) (CEILING RECESSED) | RANDOM | INDIRECT |
| | LINE ON WALL BEHIND BENCH SEATING: XENON | 0–20 LUX | LOW | VERY WARM | 0.7 M (2 FT) (WALL RECESSED) | LINEAR | INDIRECT |

**10.1** Beige: Artificial light implementation table

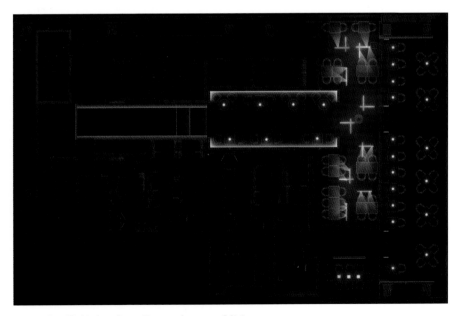

**10.2** Rendered light plan of reception area, lounge, and dining room

**10.3** Daytime view of reception area looking toward lounge: The restaurant signage is illuminated by a line of warm xenon light recessed within the wall cove. Grazing downlight, signifying a daytime condition, is visible in the lounge space beyond.

**10.4** Nighttime view of lounge looking toward reception area: The peripheral walls are grazed with uplight.

# Lounge

**10.5** View of dining room: Soft light emanates from graphic cuts in the ceiling, while accent lights provide additional illumination to individual dining tables.

The lounge is a transitional space between reception and dining, a place where such temporality finds visual representation in lighting. 10.4 By day the peripheral, fine-metal-mesh walls are lit from the ceiling and grazed by a soft, warm light, while by night these same walls are lit from the floor, resulting in a more dramatic effect. This change in light height and direction transforms the lounge into two very different spaces that cater to two different times of day and two different dining programs. The evening light, intensively concentrated at a human level, allows the upper part of the walls to dissolve in the mysterious darkness of night. The diminished height and the bodily proximity of the light sources evoke a tangibility of light that we equate with comfort and intimacy. In addition to the atmospheric wall lighting, each lounge table is also lit from the ceiling by a focused accent light that brightly illuminates the aperitifs of the culinary experience.

# Dining Room

**10.6** View of dining table in front of a perimeter horizon of light

The dining room—defined by a material palette of glass, metal, and wood—is softened through the application of warm, dim light. With the exception of accent lights focused on each table to illuminate the cuisine, light levels are kept extremely low to invoke a heightened sense of warmth and intimacy. Along the ceiling plane, graphic cuts illuminated from within add visual interest to the space. 10.5 A horizontal line of warm light recessed in a wall cove inscribes the perimeter of the dining space. This line of light defines the limits of the human level within, representing the possibility of comfort within luxury. 10.6 Furthermore, like a horizon brought within reach, this low, diffuse line of light recalls the daily phenomenon of the setting sun, and thus the dining experience is enveloped by a pervading sense of harmony, natural beauty, and calm.

# Kiasma Museum of Contemporary Art

Helsinki, Finland

Project Completion: 1998
Architect: Steven Holl Architects
Local Architect: Juhani Pallasmaa
Client: Finnish Ministry of Public Buildings

The Kiasma Museum of Contemporary Art is a building of atmospheric spaces founded from the desire to evoke a conceptual equivalence between architecture and light. 11.1–11.4 Light in this project, as in any other museographic space, is fundamental to the proper viewing and preservation of objects within. However, Kiasma is unique in that its architect, Steven Holl Architects, and lighting designer, L'Observatoire International, strove from the very beginning to make light a core part of the experience, an enhancer of spatial effects, and a revealer of architectural form. In this building the presence of light is conceived to be of equal importance to its walls, floors, and ceilings. Light is truly a malleable material through which the architectural experience is constructed.

Holl wished for all of Kiasma's lighting fixtures to be removable or concealed, so that the effects of light, and not the fixtures themselves, are what is perceived. The museum is designed to showcase an assortment of contemporary art pieces—from the most dramatic to the quietly subdued—providing a versatile backdrop in which featured pieces can be showcased to their full potential. In order to accomplish this difficult task, the architecture of light and material had to be simultaneously quiet yet powerful. Kiasma's galleries—which can be found on the second, third, and fifth floors of the museum—vary in form, and a balance of natural and electric light permeates throughout. The even, diffuse glow admitted into the exhibition rooms illuminates the volumes of space and art held within, creating an open and airy place of perceptual clarity.

While both natural and electric light are employed in the gallery spaces, one source does not attempt to overcompensate for the other as light levels shift throughout the course of the day. Instead, brightness, colors, tones, and textures within are in a constant state of flux, generating numerous experiences and readings of the space and work within. One can revisit the same painting four different times in a single day, and as the light changes, the view does too. Likewise, the gallery experience differs greatly throughout the calendar year. The geographic positioning of Helsinki—at latitude 60 degrees north, near the Arctic Circle—causes great extremes of natural daylight. In the summer the city is illuminated for close to twenty-four hours a day, while in the winter it conversely experiences nearly constant darkness. While electric lights are relied upon more heavily to properly illuminate the art and gallery spaces in the winter, out of sheer programmatic necessity, their visual impact is moderated so as not to detract from the subtle changes in natural light that still permeate throughout. This concept of movement and change, embraced fully by both architect and lighting designer, challenges traditional notions of museographic lighting, where illumination is usually static and uniform. Even with the integration of natural daylight, architects often rely on electric light to stabilize light levels in order to preserve a specific quality of desired light. L'Observatoire's approach to lighting differs, in that we embrace the temporality and nuances of natural light in order to create a richer and more spatially diverse experience. Below we describe how this balance of natural and electric light is technically achieved, and to what effect, in three different gallery spaces of the museum.

## Second-floor Galleries

The second-floor gallery spaces are small and rather rectilinear in form, with the exception of a single curved wall that defines the interior perimeter. Ceiling coves running the longitudinal length of both the inner and outer walls provide general diffuse light. The outer perimeter cove—or lighting pocket, as it came to be known—admits natural daylight, while that of the inner perimeter contains fluorescent light. 11.5 and 11.6 Because both natural and man-

| | LIGHT SOURCE | ILLUMINANCE | LUMINANCE | COLOR | HEIGHT | DENSITY | DIRECTION / DISTRIBUTION |
|---|---|---|---|---|---|---|---|
| **2ND FLOOR GALLERIES** | LIGHT POCKETS: FLUORESCENT | 20–250 LUX | MEDIUM | WARM | 4M (13 FT) | LINEAR | INDIRECT MULTIDIREC. DIFFUSE |
| | ACCENT LIGHT: HALOGEN | 0–1000 LUX | MEDIUM | WARM | 4M (13 FT) | ORGANIZED PATTERN | DIRECT DOWN CONCENTRATED |
| **3RD FLOOR GALLERIES** | LIGHT POCKETS: FLUORESCENT | 20–250 LUX | MEDIUM | WARM | 4.7 M (15 FT) | LINEAR | INDIRECT MULTIDIREC. DIFFUSE |
| | ACCENT LIGHT: HALOGEN | 0–1000 LUX | MEDIUM | WARM | 4.7 M (15 FT) | ORGANIZED PATTERN | DIRECT DOWN CONCENTRATED |
| **5TH FLOOR GALLERIES** | SKY LIGHT: FLUORESCENT | 20–100 LUX | MEDIUM | WARM | 8 M (26 FT) | LINEAR | INDIRECT MULTIDIREC. DIFFUSE |
| | INDIRECT LIGHT ON TOP OF WALL: FLUORESCENT | 20–200 LUX | MEDIUM | WARM | 5 M (16 FT) | LINEAR | INDIRECT MULTIDIREC. DIFFUSE |
| | ACCENT LIGHT: HALOGEN | 0–1000 LUX | MEDIUM | WARM | 7 M (23 FT) | ORGANIZED PATTERN | DIRECT DOWN CONCENTRATED |

**11.1** Kiasma Museum of Contemporary Art: Artificial light implementation table

**11.4** Exterior view of the museum and its urban context

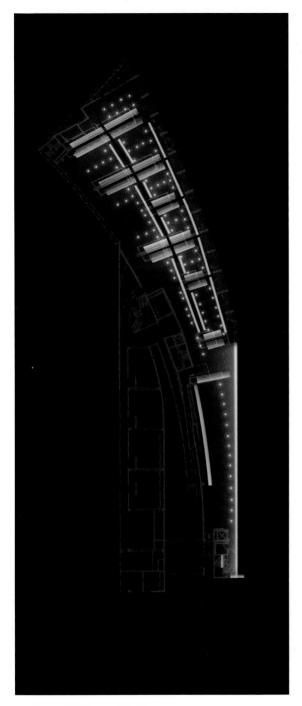

**11.2** Rendered light plan of third floor

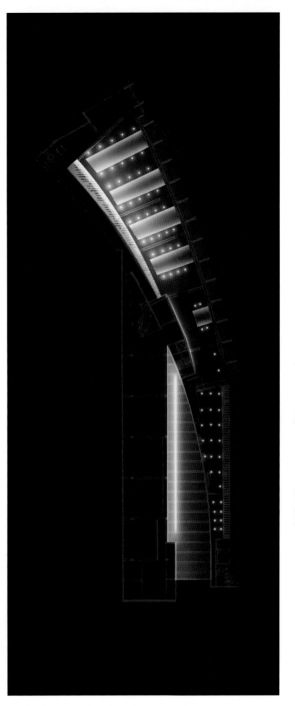

**11.3** Rendered light plan of fifth floor

**11.5** Second-floor gallery space

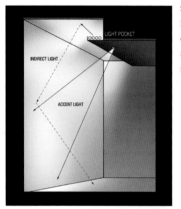

**11.6** A sectional diagram illustrates the effects of the light pocket and accent lights in a gallery space.

**11.7** Ceiling-mounted mono-point jack attachment system with halogen downlights

## Third-floor Galleries

made light sources are concealed within the pockets, the resultant light is indirect, and the atmosphere diffuse and airy (daylight is bounced off a light shelf into the space, while the fluorescent fixtures uplight a baffle that then in return bounces light back into the space). Because this light seeps in from the seams of the architecture, the ceiling planes seemingly float above, giving a tranquil feel to the space. The low illuminance levels of the indirect pockets (ranging from 20–250 lux) provide a comfortable ambient light for the galleries while simultaneously ensuring the preservation of the artwork within. The white plaster surfaces of the walls reflect and disperse the admitted light and appear themselves to glow from within.

In order to provide additional lighting for proper viewing of the artwork if necessary, a secondary system of illumination was conceived for the ceilings of the gallery spaces. A grid of mono-point jack fittings—an interchangeable fixture-mounting detail consisting of low-voltage connectors—was installed on ceiling surfaces, allowing accent downlights to be affixed where needed, moved, and replaced as exhibitions evolve and the location or type of artwork changes. 11.7 The halogen downlights, when aimed properly, provide a concentrated beam of light that illuminates each artwork with specificity and purpose. The illuminance levels of these dimmable accent lights can range from 0–1,000 lux, and can be adjusted to address the preservation needs of each artwork. The color rendering index is near 100 to ensure the proper presentation of the artist's intended coloration.

The lighting employed throughout the third-floor galleries is much like that of the second-floor galleries, but is subtly adjusted to address the formal differences of the architecture. 11.8 On the third floor, the natural lighting pocket runs the length

**11.8** Third-floor gallery space

of the longitudinal outer wall, and the man-made lighting pocket is along the longitudinal inner wall. A series of transverse walls separating gallery spaces present an opportunity to install a third typology of light pockets not found in the second-floor galleries. These transverse pockets are illuminated with fluorescent lights that again generate indirect-diffuse light that seeps into the gallery spaces between the planar seams. Because the lighting pockets start at ceiling height and extend beyond, this light source draws visitors' eyes up to the limits of the space, and in the process they discover the subtle curves of the walls and the interplay of material light that define the architectural experience. Accent lighting is integrated into the space through the same flexible ceiling mono-point jack system employed in the second-floor galleries.

**11.9** Fifth-floor gallery space

# Fifth-floor Galleries

The fifth-floor gallery contains a series of skylights installed into the curved ceiling plane, presenting the visitor with visual access to the source of natural daylight and to views of the arctic sky. 11.9 These screened skylights present abstract pieces of the sky rendered as rectangles of glowing light, framed by the white surface of the plaster ceiling. Within the skylight's perimeter walls, concealed fluorescent tubes give extra luminosity and depth to the light pockets while simultaneously providing additional indirect-diffuse light to the gallery spaces. 11.10 The skylights—as composites of natural and electric light—are the gallery's primary source of ambient light, and their height and luminosity command attention. An additional lighting cove running the length of the interior wall provides a secondary source of ambient light in the space. The overlapping rows of fluorescent tubes concealed within the discreet shelf provide uniform illumination to the perimeter walls, and a mono-point jack system for accent lighting is affixed to the exterior perimeter of the skylights.

**11.10** View of fifth-floor gallery skylight during fluorescent tube installation, prior to installation of light-diffusing screen

# Guthrie Theater

Minneapolis, Minnesota, United States

Project Completion: 2006

Architect: Ateliers Jean Nouvel

Local Architect: Architectural Alliance

Client: Guthrie Theater

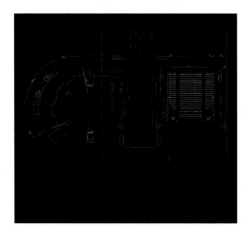

**12.1** Fourth-floor plan

**12.2** Rendered light plan of fourth floor (detail)

## Entrance Lobby

Situated on the banks of the Mississippi, at the very core of Minneapolis's historic Mill District, the Guthrie Theater celebrates the fabrication and performance of theatrical spectacle in a city founded in a culture of production. 12.1–12.4 Like the buildings of its surrounding landscape, which harness the power of water to operate as machines for agrarian production, the Guthrie Theater uses the power of the human imagination to produce its own kind of images and experiences. The Guthrie boasts 3 types of theaters within its 25,500-square-meter (275,000-square-foot) enclosure, including an 1,100-seat thrust theater, a 700-seat proscenium theater, and a 200-seat studio and experimental theater. These performance spaces are unified by a vertical chasm that slices through the assembly of volumetric forms. Within this chasm, one finds spaces for circulation and congregation that service both the viewing of theater and the view of the surrounding industrial landscape. A 53-meter-long (175-foot-long) cantilevered bridge protrudes from the vertical void, presenting the visitor with a cinematic approach to city views as a preface to the theatrical experience.

The Guthrie's lighting design heightens the theatrical drama of the architecture and the experience within, revealing the many layers of depth and darkness in Nouvel's spatial composition. The stage-like qualities of the lighting drive the experiential trajectory, forming an alternative narrative unveiled in tandem with that of the architecture. From the exterior on in, the visitor is led through a sequence of progressively darker spaces, culminating in the entrance into one of the theaters. Here we analyze one such trajectory through the vertical chasm—from the entrance lobby through to the proscenium stage—to illustrate the application of lighting.

The entrance to the first-floor building lobby is marked by a flood of light demarcating the threshold between

| | LIGHT SOURCE | ILLUMINANCE | LUMINANCE | COLOR | HEIGHT | DENSITY | DIRECTION / DISTRIBUTION |
|---|---|---|---|---|---|---|---|
| ENTRANCE LOBBY | ENTRANCE LIGHTING : HALOGEN | 0–150 LUX | LOW | WARM | 10 M (35 FT) (CEILING RECESSED) | 1.5 M (5 FT) O.C. ORGANIZED PATTERN | DIRECT DOWN CONCENTRATED |
| | TRACK DOWNLIGHTS ON UNDERSIDE OF 2ND FLOOR VOLUME: HALOGEN | 0–200 LUX | LOW | WARM | 5 M (16 FT) (CEILING MOUNTED) | 2 M (6 FT) O.C. ORGANIZED PATTERN | DIRECT DOWN CONCENTRATED |
| | DISPLAY SYSTEM UPLIGHT: HALOGEN | 0–150 LUX | LOW | WARM | 2 M (6 FT) | ORGANIZED PATTERN | UP DIFFUSE |
| 4TH FLOOR FOYER | LIGHT FROM BEHIND BENCH: FLUORESCENT | 50 LUX | LOW | WARM | 0 M (0 FT) (FLOOR MOUNTED) | LINEAR | UP DIFFUSE |
| | GENERAL LIGHTING FROM CEILING: LOW-VOLTAGE HALOGEN | 0–100 LUX | MEDIUM | WARM | 2.5M (8 FT) (CEILING RECESSED) | ORGANIZED PATTERN (LINEAR AXIS) | DIRECT DOWN CONCENTRATED |
| | GLOWING PLANE OF LIGHT IN CEILING CUT: COLD CATHODE | N/A | HIGH | WARM | 2.6–6 M (8 FT–20 FT) (BTW FLOORS) | LINEAR | MULTIDIREC. DIFFUSE |
| | GLOWING RAMP WALL: COLD CATHODE | N/A | HIGH | WARM / RED | 1–2.75 M (3 FT–9 FT) (ABOVE RAMP) | LINEAR | MULTIDIREC. DIFFUSE |
| ACCESS TO PROSCENIUM THEATER / STAIRWELL | GENERAL LIGHTING FROM CEILING: HALOGEN | 100 LUX | LOW | WARM | 9 M (30 FT) (CEILING RECESSED) | RANDOM | DIRECT DOWN CONCENTRATED |
| | UPLIGHT ATOP WALL: FLUORESCENT | 50 LUX | MEDIUM | WARM + COLOR GEL | 8 M (26 FT) | LINEAR | INDIRECT UP |
| | EXPOSED LIGHT TUBES ALONG STAIRWELL PERIMETER: INCANDESCENT | 100 LUX | HIGH | WARM | EVERY 2.8 M (9 FT) (BTW LANDINGS) | LINEAR | DIFFUSE |
| PROSCENIUM THEATER | HOUSE LIGHTING: HALOGEN FRAMING PROJECTOR | 0–300 LUX | LOW | WARM | 5-6.5 M (16–21 FT) (IN CEILING CATWALK) | ORGANIZED PATTERN (BTW BAFFLES) | DIRECT DOWN CONCENTRATED |
| | WALL-WASHING UPLIGHT ON METALLIC CURTAIN: HALOGEN | N/A | MEDIUM | RED | 0 M (0 FT) (FLOOR MOUNTED | LINEAR | DIRECT UP |

**12.3** Guthrie Theater: Artificial light implementation table

exterior and interior, the everyday and the theatrical. Like the curtains of a proscenium stage, these concentrated downlights—recessed into the four-story-high ceiling—cascade light, illuminating the entrance with dramatic flair. The low luminance levels enable a visitor to cross this visual threshold comfortably, and the warm light makes the lobby an inviting place. Once inside, the lobby—which accommodates displays and ticket sales—is predominantly lit during the day by the natural light that floods in through the lobby's full-height glass walls. By night track

**12.4** Exterior view of the Guthrie Theater: A concentrated beam of light cast upon the entrance pavement demarcates the experiential transition into the theatrical realm.

**12.5** Fourth-floor foyer: View looking away from bridge

mounted downlights affixed to the bottom perimeter of the suspended office volume and uplights mounted on top of the moveable signage walls create a dynamic atmosphere within. The downlights act as accent lights, illuminating the pathway through the space, while the case-mounted uplights provide ambient light for the general spatial experience. The light emanating from the top of these independent volumes also illuminates faint illustrations of great artists and performers hanging along the longitudinal walls that appear and disappear in the soft glow of the warm light, like ghosts of a theatrical past.

## Fourth-floor Foyer

By means of escalators located along the perimeter walls of the entrance lobby, a visitor travels from the first floor to the fourth-floor foyer, an overflow gathering space for pre- and post-show entertainment and an access point to the proscenium theater. This long, corridorlike space is capped on one end by blue-tinted glass and on the other by the projection of the vista bridge, a ramp that guides visitors up to the fifth-floor cafe. 12.5 The walls of the fourth-floor foyer are lined with benches that have light emanating from behind them. Floor-mounted linear fluorescents running the length of the benches cast a soft, warm glow upon the vertical walls, which is decorated with ghostlike images of performers. The 2.5-meter-high (8.5-foot-tall) ceiling is sliced by a central axis of track-mounted downlights, aimed to illuminate the passageway beneath. Because each downlight shines at a slightly different angle, a syncopated pattern of light is projected along the center of the floor surface. The areas of light, reminiscent of theatrical spotlights, articulate a playful rhythm along the length of the corridor, which visually culminates in a large circular projection of warm, white light, shining from a cut in the ceiling. This opening—which mediates between the fourth-floor foyer and fifth-floor cafe—is a monumental form in an otherwise rectilinear space and marks the spatial transition from the interior of the building to the cantilevered bridge. The warm, white light emanating from within is produced by a diffuse plane of cold-cathode tubes surrounded by stretch fabric. From the opposite end of the corridor looking toward the bridge, the seemingly random yet linear pattern of downlights cast upon the floor guides one's eyes in axis to the brighter, whiter light of the circular opening, and ultimately to the intense blue rectangle of light capping the end of the cantilever bridge.

## Bridge Access to the Fifth-floor Cafe

A cantilevered bridge to the fifth floor acts as both a circulation route and an observation point within the theater's general organization. The ascent up the switchback ramp permits the visitor access to the theater's bar and cafe through a truly unique spatial sequence of forms, images, and vistas. Because the climax of this sequence is truly the view of the industrial city from the window of the ramp's viewing platform, illumination levels were kept at a minimum in order to emphasize this monumental place. The ramp's central dividing wall is lit with cold-cathode light, rendering it a powerful, singular volume visually capable of splitting the mass of the floor. By day this wall appears white so as not to detract from the intense blue light emanating from the tinted glass window. At night, however, the dividing wall glows a dramatic red as a preface to the color and intensity of lighting conditions to be experienced within the theater. 12.6 and 12.7

**12.6 and 12.7** Daytime (left) and nighttime (right) views from the bridge ramp

## Staircase and Hallway between the Fourth and Fifth Floors

A staircase situated outside the lobby's perimeter walls in the zone between gathering space and theater provides alternative access from the fifth-floor cafe to the proscenium theater, in lieu of the ramp. The lighting of this stairwell aims to mentally prepare the visitor for the theatrical experience through the

**12.8** Theater access stairwells: Staircase landings are marked by exposed linear incandescent lamps.

**12.9** Theater access corridor: Recessed cove uplighting draws attention to the verticality of the space.

reduction of light levels and exposure to the color red as a preface to the dramatic experience that awaits. The vertical stairwell openings between landings are lined with exposed incandescent tubes. 12.8 These warm lights of high luminance articulate the rectilinear openings of the stairwell, rendering perimeter definition. In the corridor between stairwell and theater, randomly spaced halogen downlights recessed into the ceiling subtly illuminate the passageway, accentuating the deep red color of the carpet below. A cove between wall and ceiling running the length of the corridor is uplit with fluorescent white light that aims to emphasize the verticality of the space, enabling the ceiling to visually float. 12.9

## Proscenium Theaters

**12.10** Interior of the proscenium theater

Upon entrance into the proscenium theater, the visitor finds himself enveloped in a cavernous space saturated in a deep red color. 12.10 In order to make this space both functional and experientially powerful, two main types of lighting are employed. First, halogen framing projectors disguised behind architectural baffles in the ceiling of the auditorium serve as the primary house lighting, their effect perceived on the myriad of red surfaces they illuminate. These fixtures cast direct light upon the seats and corridors, ensuring adequate visibility and the illumination of the overall space. Moreover, the white light they shed makes visitors appear normal in the otherwise red-lit space. The lights can be dimmed or increased to signal the beginning or end of the performance. Second, halogen uplights tinted with red glass subtly graze the metallic, curtain-sheathed walls along the perimeter of the theater. As a result, the periphery is rendered in deep red light, which is in turn reflected and dispersed into the greater space of the auditorium.

# Essays

# A Conversation with Steven Holl

October 14, 2009

**Hervé Descottes:** How do architecture and space make use of light?

**Steven Holl:** Space is oblivion without light. A building speaks through the silence of perception orchestrated by light. Luminosity is as integral to its spatial experience as porosity is integral to urban experience.

For our Helsinki Museum of Contemporary Art, Kiasma, the most important building material was light. Of the twenty-five galleries that make up the main function of the museum, all have a slice of natural light. The behavior of light guided many decisions. The low angle of the Helsinki sun, never reaching above 51 degrees, helps give sectional form to the curved, "light-catching" aspect of the architecture. Changes in natural lighting conditions are left visible—so passing clouds bring shadow, and brightness varies as the interior experience varies.

The exterior of Kiasma lacks conventional lighting—the building glows from within, projecting its own light outward. The Nelson-Atkins Museum of Art in Kansas City, a competition-winning project in 1999 that opened in 2007, takes this idea of night luminosity to the extent that at night the building seems to be completely constructed out of luminous material. Appearing as luminous shards of glass in the landscape, the "lenses" form courtyard sculpture gardens. 13.1

**13.1** Steven Holl Architects (architect) and Renfro Design Group (lighting consultant), Nelson-Atkins Museum of Art, Kansas City, Missouri, 2007: By night, the buildings glow from within. The perceived materiality of built form and light become one and the same.

**HD:** What is the relationship between artificial and natural light in architecture?

**SH:** Sometimes we try to integrate the source points of natural light and artificial light. Working together on the Kiasma galleries, this was the intention. The twenty-five galleries in the building have a range of sizes, but all have natural light, and at these geometric cuts, the artificial light appears when the sun goes down.

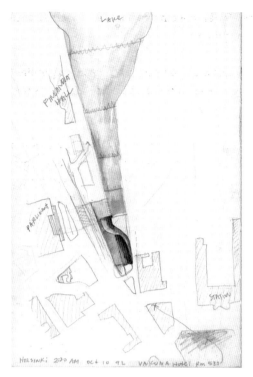

**13.2** Steven Holl, Kiasma Museum of Contemporary Art, Helsinki, Finland, 1992: Concept plan

**13.3** Hand-rendering of an interior public space in the Kiasma Museum

HD: At what point do you begin to conceive of light in your design process and in what ways?

SH: We conceive of the space, light, and concept of a work from the very beginning. Often in concept watercolors, the aspects of light are there in the first sketch, integral to the concept of the architecture, unique to the site and place. 13.2 – 13.4

HD: What is the role of the lighting designer in collaborations?

SH: Often the lighting designer—you—is part of the design collaborations from the very beginning. We have pin-up critique sessions on the various

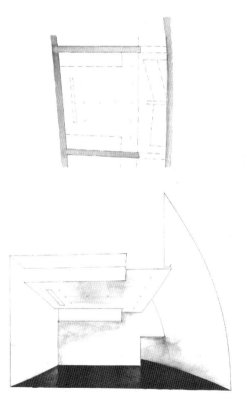

**13.4** Hand-rendering of plan and an interior public space in the Kiasma Museum

**13.5** Steven Holl Architects (architect) and Renfro Design Group (lighting consultant), New York University Department of Philosophy, New York, New York, 2007: Interior view of staircase illuminated by skylight

**13.6** Under the right conditions, a prismatic film installed on the south-facing window of the stairwell skylight in the New York University Department of Philosophy breaks the sunlight into a prismatic rainbow.

schemes for an ongoing competition together with many consultants.

HD: How do you negotiate the effects of light with the presence or concealment of the fixtures that generate this light?

SH: Each project is different, however in our museum spaces we have often managed to integrate the natural and artificial light sources with the geometry of the space in order to conceal the sources. We have aimed for washes of light that emanate from the folds in space.

HD: Are you ever surprised by the effects of lighting on your architecture?

SH: The surprising things about light are often experiences in seasonal changes or daily changes. For example at the New York University Department of Philosophy, the prismatic light in the main stair only occurs at certain times of the day. Suddenly there might be a burst of prismatically refracted color washing the walls and stairs. 13.5 and 13.6

The infinite possibilities of light have been evident from the beginning of architecture and will continue into the future. The revelations of new spaces, like interwoven languages, dissolve and reappear in light. In magnificent spaces, light changes and appears to describe form. An eclipse of white clarity suddenly gives way to a pulse with color; light is contingent, its shadows intermittent.

# Sensations of Light

Sylvain Dubuisson

A lighting project is founded in an architectural intention, one that responds to individual programs as diverse as a boutique, a restaurant, a private residence, or a museum, each with a style whose breadth can range from minimalism to deconstruction.

One can ask light to integrate itself into a space or expose itself indirectly by means of reflection from surfaces or absorption into glowing objects. These traits can be exclusive or combined. Light can give sequence and identity to a space, and can be employed to emphasize material effects.

Artificial light, together or apart from natural daylight, can open infinite possibilities. However, one must have the scientific knowledge to properly orchestrate these sources in order to respond to aesthetic and technical requirements, to push limits, to provoke impressions beyond what we are accustomed to in such a way that affects our senses in a natural, subtle, or surprising manner.

The variety of sources, their multitude of combined effects, the search for a sensitive balance that can provoke emotion—all of these factors come together in a complex manner that necessitates the artful skill of orchestration with extreme distinction.

Light is both nothing and everything. Light is nothing: it is untouchable, it moves, it travels, it is but a fleeting stroke in the immaterial world. Light is everything: it alone brings space into reality, limited or unlimited, visible or simply intuited.

**14.1** Sylvain Dubuisson, *Plafonnier à plumes* (1998): This fixture was designed for the rural property of Monsieur G., situated in a landscape of limestone rocks beside a body of water that ducks call their home. On the ground floor of Monsieur G.'s home, a collection of photographic portraits is housed along the length of a corridor. The *Plafonnier à plumes* was specifically designed to illuminate this gallery, and three are employed along its length in alternating rhythm with the gallery's windows. Two leaves of translucent paper—oriented parallel to the walls—surround each fixture's lightbulb, softening the emitted light and reducing the incidence of glare upon the photographs displayed. Perpendicular to these leaves and on axis with the corridor, suspended duck feathers collected from the property's grounds further filter the light, evoking the spirit of the site.

# Light and Landscape

James Corner

Regardless of their specific medium, artists know that light is the essential element for bringing the world to life. With the right source, angle, intensity, and quality of light, the reception of even the most ordinary object or environment can be heightened to an almost transcendental level of presence and effect. While the practice of lighting typically entails spot-lighting and highlighting, the greater poetry of lighting involves atmosphere, ambience, and background, recognizing the inevitable coexistence and interplay of light with shadow and darkness. The technique of chiaroscuro in drawing and painting, for example, renders gradients of light to bring shape, definition, and poetic presence to a figure. Such gradients may sometimes be abrupt, sharp, and in contrast, and at other times, grade subtly across a range of tones. Add color and temperature to tonal range, and an infinite series of possibilities emerges for creating memorable presence, mood, and character. Light not only brings things to life, but also recasts how the ordinary world can be seen, in fresh and different ways; hence, the power of art.

Painters, photographers, and stage-set designers have long understood the revelatory power of light and the subsequent necessity to precisely control it in their work, utilizing extraordinarily disciplined and precise techniques to create certain moods and qualities—sometimes exuberant, sometimes restrained. Architects too have historically been sensitive to how light reveals exterior form and penetrates an interior, bringing particular shape, mood, and quality to space. Precise geometry, construction, and materials control and nuance the desired qualities of light, and can be particularly effective when tuned to the peculiarities of place (Nordic light as distinct from Brazilian for example, one softly bright with pallid shadows, the other intensely bright with sharp, deep dark recesses).

With regard to landscapes and exterior spaces, light is fundamental to the character and quality of a

**15.1** Albert Bierstadt, *Sierra Nevada Morning* (1870), (from the collection of the Gilcrease Museum, Tulsa, Oklahoma)

**15.2** The Isle of the Meadows, late afternoon, Fresh Kills (2000)

place. Landscapes literally come into being through light, and the play of light is extremely specific to location and environment, irreproducible elsewhere and inspiring scores of local artists for centuries—the big skies and moody weather of Jacob van Ruisdael and John Constable; the atmospheric, misty drama of J. M. W. Turner; the impressive sublime of Albert Bierstadt and photographer Ansel Adams; or the temporal theatricality of landscape in the films of Zhang Yimou (*Hero*, 2002), for example. 15.1

In each case, not only is landscape a massive medium revealed through light and shadow, but it is also a medium through which light itself is brought to an inexorable presence. This presenting and revealing of light is familiar in both architecture and landscape architecture, wherein specific topographic and material configurations elevate light to heightened (and sometimes novel) levels of reception. The architect Richard Meier believes in white buildings because whiteness allows the local color and light to appear. Similarly, great landscapes—through ground modulation, plantings, water bodies, and other designed elements—capture and reveal local light in new and transformative ways. It is not just that light and shadow are showcasing the landscape, but more that the landscape is actualizing light itself, rendering light in new ways, light that would be immaterial without a surface—or field of textures—to make it visible in a particular way.

One of the most exciting aspects of lighting and landscape is that they are both subject to the passages of time: early-morning dawn colors the land in a particular way, often with very striking colors, shortening shadows and increasing clarity. The morning is very different from midday, which tends to wash things out; dawn is echoed again, albeit differently, with the late afternoon's lengthening shadows, warm sunset tones, and the atmospheric, thickening hues of dusk. Even nighttime has a certain character of light—dim, even dark, but once the eyes have

adjusted, there is just enough definition to make out blackened forms and space. And, of course, the different seasons bring about different characters of light: summer has warm, vibrant, saturated tones; fall is melancholic and shadowy; winter light is typically a little harsh and sometimes bright; and spring harbors an increasingly luminescent, clear, fresh light. These different kinds of light enrich the experiential range of a landscape, allowing for varied forms of appreciation and understanding, and in turn, the landscape reveals the shifting beauty of local light and the passages of time.

Landscapes and buildings are not only subject to the play of natural light, but are also enhanced through artificial light. Historically, artificial light came from flames (candles, torches, and fires), creating wonderfully flickering penumbras that were simultaneously bright and shadowy, scented, warm, and tactile. Today, with electricity, there are myriad forms of artificial lighting used to light buildings and landscapes. Unfortunately, many contemporary lighting schemes are all about the light, not the space or the place, and most fail to evoke any poetic or imaginative affect. Contemporary lighting is often overly bright, too white, and more about fixture and light source than the illuminated object or space. There is a subtle but definite art to understanding how to conceive and deploy artificial light: learning from the behavior and peculiarities of natural light, the specificity of local conditions, and the repertoire of material techniques to render both light and shadow in beautiful ways. The art of light requires an appreciation of darkness, shadow, and atmosphere, out of which light appears—a phenomenology of luminosity, not simply a practice of spotlighting.

# Fresh Kills Park

Staten Island, New York, United States

Fresh Kills Park is an ongoing project to transform more than 2,200 acres of closed landfill on Staten Island into a new public park. 15.2 With the construction of paths, roads, and park spaces, the area will need to be lit with artificial lighting, especially from dusk to dawn. The site is massive in scale, and is significant because of its openness in contrast to the context of surrounding urban development. The site is also significant as a nature reserve, offering large spaces for flocks of migrating birds, as well as habitats for nesting, breeding, and feeding. For these reasons, we felt that the site should be dark at nighttime, a sort of protective void nested within the metropolitan grid of light.

Working with Hervé Descottes, we developed an approach toward lighting the site to meet minimal requirements only, and focused on lighting edges rather than whole areas. For example, instead of light being focused upon paths and roads, the light is turned to illuminate the edge landscape. Car headlights can adequately see the road surface, and the eye can clearly see the way with the landscape edges being highlighted. And on pedestrian paths, the eye adjusts to follow the luminescent landscape edge rather than feeling enclosed by a dark landscape on an overly bright path. Similarly, lighting fixtures are designed to themselves be minimal, with the light source hidden so that the only light visible is that absorbed and reflected by the landscape. This approach is significant in that it seeks to minimize the intrusion of artificial light on a largely natural setting, protecting habitats for birds and animals while recognizing how the dark light of the night can actually increase an elemental sense of natural expanse, of void and diurnal time.

# High Line

New York, New York, United States

The High Line is a former freight rail line—elevated thirty feet above the street and running for nearly a mile and a half through the urban fabric of Manhattan's west side—that has been transformed into a spectacular new urban public promenade, a strolling garden in the sky. 15.3 A large part of the experiential drama of walking along the High Line derives from its detached and elevated character, affording unusual glimpses and panoramas into and across the city. The city becomes the landscape, the shifting scenery revealed through a carefully designed choreography of movement. In the evening and into the nighttime hours, the transition from daylight to the switching on of the illuminated city—the multitude of lit windows, building facades, streets, and signs—is particularly dramatic, with the city providing a beautiful tapestry of ambient light.

In considering the lighting design for the High Line with Hervé Descottes, we determined that we needed to keep the light low on the High Line—low in height (below eye level) and low in intensity—in order for the city light to be visible. Raised lighting fixtures would only wash out the background, making the city dark, and too high of a light intensity would prevent the retina from tuning into the ambient light of the city. The solution was to hide the light source (a continuous strip of LED lights) in the side railing at forty-two inches high (just above the waist) and cast a soft area of light onto the planting and paving, marking the edge with light (as with Fresh Kills) rather than the whole area. Again, the visitor does not see light as much as they see strangely luminous grasses, glowing flowers, and textural landscape, all of which is set into a sequence of movement and duration. And the city light beyond is magnificent!

**15.3** View of the High Line walkway with floating benches

In both of these instances, the technicality of the lighting design is very complicated and precise, and yet the result is often extremely simple, understated, and more a form of background ambience than a foreground feature in and of itself. Lighting in the landscape creates a mood, an atmosphere, an imaginative effect—a feeling that is powerful and lasting, but without self-consciousness or showy extravagance. Landscape after all is not an object to be highlighted, but a field, a texture of duration, passage, and elemental connectedness with nature. Light brings landscape to life, but landscape may also reveal new potentialities of both lightness and darkness as phenomenal expressions of space, place, and time.

# Appendices

A lighting designer is generally responsible for providing both the conceptual approach to the lighting of a given space as well as the technical analysis necessary for its successful execution. At the middle to advanced stages of the lighting design process, lighting designers work closely with architects and engineers to generate a series of technical documents that describe the proposed lighting scheme and its visual consequences. Documents of particular importance in this process are lighting-fixture layouts, generated on architectural plans, and reflected ceiling plans (RCPs) and illuminance calculations based on the proposed luminaire layouts. Other probable documents issued include renderings, digital models, sections, detail sketches of lighting conditions, and lighting fixture schedules. In order to better explain the role of these documents in the context of an architectural design project, we have included several technical drawings of the Dundas Walkway in the Art Gallery of Ontario in Toronto, Canada (Gehry Partners, LLP), for reference. The limited scale of the space and the clarity of lighting intent make these drawings particularly legible to all, and good exemplars of their type. 16.1

A lighting fixture layout locates all proposed fixtures on the RCP or plan drawing following a coding logic established by the lighting designer (see Appendix E for an example of such a legend). In turn, an illuminance calculation provides both a visual and a numerical understanding of the specified luminaires' effect within a space. Illuminance calculations such as the ones pictured in Figure 16.2 are generated by computer programs that calculate the total luminaire lumens per area (considering light loss and/or room utilization factors) according to their placement and aiming within a three-dimensional digital model. The photometric data results show illuminance values (indicated by the field of red numbers) as well as contour lines for constant light values (demarcated as pink, blue, and green contour lines). Color-rendered photometric diagrams are an alternate form of visual

# LIGHTING FIXTURE LAYOUT AND ILLUMINANCE CALCULATIONS

## LIGHTING FIXTURE LAYOUT

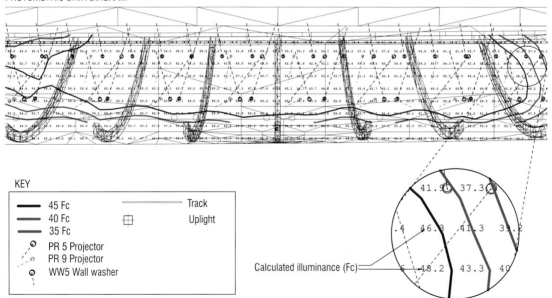

Specified uplight (UL1)

Specified track (TR3A) for installment of fixtures:
Projectors (PR5, PR9) and wall washer (WW5)

## PHOTOMETRIC DATA DIAGRAM

### KEY

| | |
|---|---|
| 45 Fc | Track |
| 40 Fc | Uplight |
| 35 Fc | |
| PR 5 Projector | |
| PR 9 Projector | |
| WW5 Wall washer | |

Calculated illuminance (Fc)

## NUMERIC SUMMARY

| Label | Calculation Type | Units | Average | Maximum | Minimum | Average / Minimum | Maximum / Minimum |
|---|---|---|---|---|---|---|---|
| Floor | Illuminance | Fc | 54.89 | 69.5 | 13.8 | 3.98 | 5.04 |
| Wall (not pictured) | Illuminance | Fc | 29.74 | 40.2 | 15.3 | 1.94 | 2.63 |

**16.2** Gehry Partners, LLP, Dundas Walkway, Art Gallery of Ontario,

Toronto, Canada: Lighting fixture layout and illuminance calculations

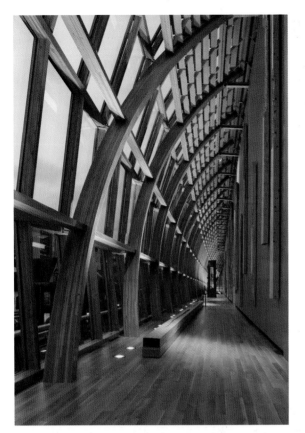

representation, conveying the same information as the photometric data diagram. 16.3 The purpose of these plan and elevation diagrams (which can be generated simultaneously) is to ensure that required or desired illuminance levels are achieved. In addition to providing illuminance data, computer programs can also provide rendered images of the effects of a proposed lighting scheme within the given space. 16.4

**16.1** View of the completed Dundas Walkway corridor

**16.4** Rendering of artificial corridor lighting for the Dundas Walkway

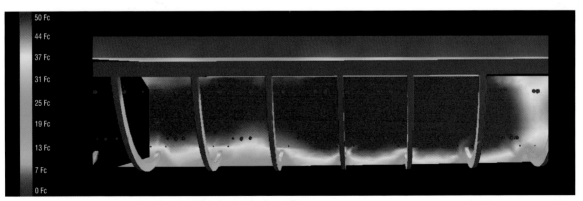

**16.3** Color-rendered photometric plan of artificial light for the Dundas Walkway

# HISTORICAL TIMELINE OF LIGHT SOURCES*

| Year | Source Type |
|------|-------------|

**3000 BCE**
- Fire
- Candles
- Oil lamps

**500 BCE**

**1800**
- Electric arc lamp demonstrated
- Gas lamp
- Edison invents the electric lamp

**1900**

**1910**
- Indirect lighting demonstrated
- Neon lamp demonstrated

**1920**

**1930**
- Mercury vapor lamp introduced
- Reflector lamp introduced
- Fluorescent lamp introduced

**1940**
- Parabolic aluminized reflector (PAR) lamp introduced

**1950**

**1960**
- Tungsten halogen lamp introduced
- High-pressure sodium (HPS) lamp introduced
- First practical visible spectrum light-emitting diodes (LEDs)
- Metal halide lamp introduced

**1970**

**1980**
- Compact fluorescent lamps introduced
- First organic LED lamp introduced
- High-frequency ballasts introduced

**1990**
- First commercial electrodeless lamps
- Commercial introduction of ceramic metal halide (MH) lamps
- First indium-gallium-nitride LEDs

**2000**
- RGB technology introduced
- Solid state plasma introduced

**2010**

*Partial information based on "Timeline of Light Sources" in Mark S. Rea, ed., *The IESNA Lighting Handbook: Reference & Application*, 9th ed. (New York: Illuminating Engineering Society of North America, 2000).

Appendix A: Historical Timeline of Light Sources

# RECOMMENDED ILLUMINANCE VALUES*

| TASK TYPE | LUX | | | | | |
|---|---|---|---|---|---|---|
| | 50 | 100 | 500 | 1,000 | 5,000 | 10,000 |
| ORIENTATION AND SIMPLE VISUAL TASKS | | | | | | |
| Public spaces [1] | ▮ | | | | | |
| Simple orientation [2] | | ▮ | | | | |
| Occasional visual tasks [3] | | | ▮ | | | |
| COMMON VISUAL TASKS | | | | | | |
| Large visual tasks [4] | | | | ▮ | | |
| Small visual tasks [5] | | | | ▮ | | |
| Very small visual tasks [6] | | | | | ▮ | |
| SPECIAL VISUAL TASKS | | | | | | |
| Visual task near theshold [7] | | | | | ▬▬▬▬▬ | |

[1] Spaces such as inactive storage

[2] Spaces such as lobbies, corridors, elevators, stairs

[3] Spaces such as active storage, locker rooms, office lounges/reception, school auditoriums

[4] Spaces such as restrooms, general office spaces, conference rooms, classrooms

[5] Spaces such as accounting offices, science laboratories

[6] Tasks such as drafting (low contrast), lecture demonstration, or store feature displays

[7] Where supplementary task lighting is necessary, i.e., dentistry work or medical operations

* Data based on "Determination of Illuminance Categories" in Mark S. Rea, ed., *The IESNA Lighting Handbook: Reference & Application*, 9th ed. (New York: Illuminating Engineering Society of North America, 2000).

Appendix B: Recommended Illuminance Values

# COLOR TEMPERATURE VS. COLOR RENDERING INDEX OF LIGHT SOURCES

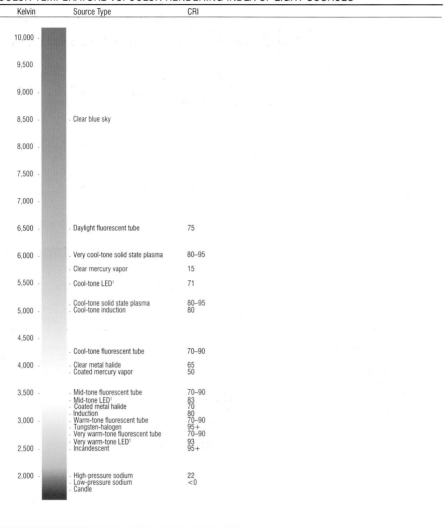

| Kelvin | Source Type | CRI |
|---|---|---|
| 10,000 | | |
| 9,500 | | |
| 9,000 | | |
| 8,500 | Clear blue sky | |
| 8,000 | | |
| 7,500 | | |
| 7,000 | | |
| 6,500 | Daylight fluorescent tube | 75 |
| 6,000 | Very cool-tone solid state plasma | 80–95 |
| | Clear mercury vapor | 15 |
| 5,500 | Cool-tone LED[1] | 71 |
| 5,000 | Cool-tone solid state plasma | 80–95 |
| | Cool-tone induction | 80 |
| 4,500 | | |
| | Cool-tone fluorescent tube | 70–90 |
| 4,000 | Clear metal halide | 65 |
| | Coated mercury vapor | 50 |
| 3,500 | Mid-tone fluorescent tube | 70–90 |
| | Mid-tone LED[1] | 83 |
| | Coated metal halide | 70 |
| | Induction | 80 |
| 3,000 | Warm-tone fluorescent tube | 70–90 |
| | Tungsten-halogen | 95+ |
| | Very warm-tone fluorescent tube | 70–90 |
| | Very warm-tone LED[1] | 93 |
| 2,500 | Incandescent | 95+ |
| 2,000 | High-pressure sodium | 22 |
| | Low-pressure sodium | <0 |
| | Candle | |

[1]Data based on U.S. Department of Energy, CALiPER Summary Report, Round 9, October 2009.

Appendix C: Color Temperature vs. Color Rendering Index of Light Sources

## BASIC CHARACTERISTICS OF GENERAL LIGHT SOURCES

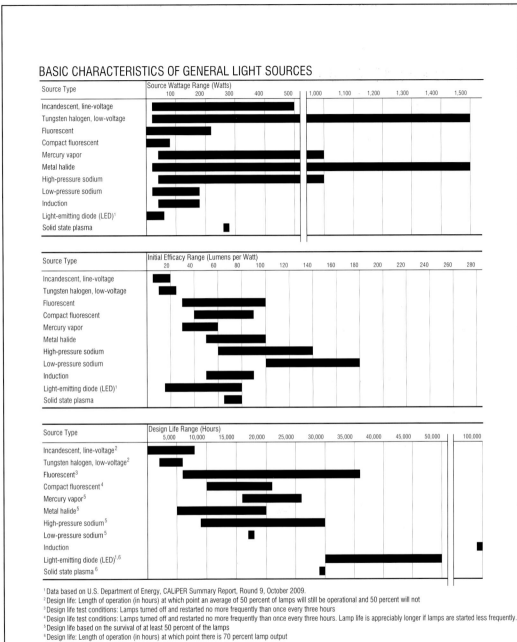

[1] Data based on U.S. Department of Energy, CALiPER Summary Report, Round 9, October 2009.
[2] Design life: Length of operation (in hours) at which point an average of 50 percent of lamps will still be operational and 50 percent will not
[3] Design life test conditions: Lamps turned off and restarted no more frequently than once every three hours
[4] Design life test conditions: Lamps turned off and restarted no more frequently than once every three hours. Lamp life is appreciably longer if lamps are started less frequently.
[5] Design life based on the survival of at least 50 percent of the lamps
[6] Design life: Length of operation (in hours) at which point there is 70 percent lamp output

Appendix D: Basic Characteristics of General Light Sources

# LIGHTING SYMBOL LEGEND

| Symbol | Name | Symbol | Name |
|---|---|---|---|
| BO_ | BOLLARD | SLE_ | STEPLIGHT EXTERIOR |
| BOE_ | BOLLARD EXTERIOR | ST_ | STRIPLIGHT |
| DL_ | DOWNLIGHT | STE_ | STRIPLIGHT EXTERIOR |
| DLE_ | DOWNLIGHT EXTERIOR | SU_ | SUBMERSIBLE |
| FL_ | FLOORLAMP | TL_ | TABLELAMP |
| PR_ | FRAMING PROJECTOR | UL_ | UPLIGHT |
| PRE_ | FRAMING PROJECTOR EXTERIOR | ULE_ | UPLIGHT EXTERIOR |
| PL_ | PENDANT | WS_ | WALLSCONCE |
| PLE_ | PENDANT EXTERIOR | WSE_ | WALLSCONCE EXTERIOR |
| POE_ | POLE LAMP | WW_ | WALLWASHER |
| SL_ | STEPLIGHT | WWE_ | WALLWASHER EXTERIOR |

Appendix E: Lighting Symbol Legend

The above lighting symbol legend provides a visual listing of commonly used luminaire types. Such symbols are employed in lighting fixture layouts to convey the location and densities of fixtures in plan.

## Glossary

**Accent lighting**

Directional lighting to emphasize or draw attention to an artifact or architectural feature

**Ambient lighting**

Lighting that provides general illumination throughout an area

**Amperage**

The electric current or the rate of flow of electrons, which is equal to wattage divided by voltage. The standard unit of measurement for electric current is the ampere.

**Baffle**

An opaque or translucent element used to control light distribution at certain angles

**Ballast**

A device for operating lamp sources such as HIDs and fluorescents that use an electric discharge or arc. The ballast provides the necessary voltage, current, and waveform for starting and operating these lamps.

**Beam-spread**

The angular cone of light in a directional photometric distribution. This angle is measured between the two outside rays, which are 50 percent of the peak or center-beam intensity.

**Bollard**

A luminaire having the appearance of a short post, used for path and area lighting

**Candela (cd)**

Unit describing the intensity of light in a specific direction, defined as one lumen per steradian. (A steradian is the unit of solid angle measuring a two-dimensional angle in three-dimensional space.)

**Chromaticity**

Describes the perceived color of light in terms of the dominant or complementary wavelength as measured on a spectral chromaticity diagram or from coordinates on the industry standard CIS chromaticity chart

**Cold-cathode**

Short for fluorescent cold-cathode, it is sometimes confused with neon, but is a form of fluorescent technology. It differs from standard fluorescent or hot-cathode, in that a higher voltage is supplied to the cathodes so they are not required to be independently heated to create a discharge. Cold-cathode is characterized by its ability to be custom-formed into curves and shapes, and has a lower efficacy but longer life than standard fluorescents.

**Color rendering**

A general expression for the ability of a light source to display colors accurately. The color rendering index (CRI) is a scale from 1 to 100 that measures the ability of a light source to render a surface color compared to a theoretical reference light source. Daylight is widely considered to be equivalent to 100 CRI.

**Color temperature**

A rating relating the overall color appearance of a white light source to a theoretical reference source, heated to a particular temperature measured in units kelvin (K). A value of 3500 K is typically described as even white light. Values below 3500 K are described as warm, and approach reddish hues, while values above 3500 K are considered cool, and approach bluish hues.

**Compact fluorescent**

A miniature fluorescent lamp characterized by a small-diameter fluorescent tube folded or curved on itself to utilize a single-ended base and reduce its overall size. These are often used as an alternative to incandescent lighting, with approximately ten times the lamp life and three to four times the efficacy.

**Contrast**

The relationship between the luminance of an object and its background

**Cove lighting**

Lighting sources that are shielded by a ledge or cove for the purpose of indirectly lighting the ceiling

**Diffuse**

Term describing a dispersed light distribution or the scattering or softening of light

**Diffuse source**

A lamp or luminaire that emits light from a perceptible broad surface with a distribution characterized as dispersed light. Diffuse light sources will tend to soften shadows and are perceived as less dramatic. They are typically described in contrast with a linear source or point source.

**Diffuser**

A lens or material that shields the light source in a fixture, used to redirect and scatter the light distribution or decrease the luminosity by increasing the visible surface area

**Direct lighting**

Lighting involving luminaires that distribute most of their light toward a task surface, typically downward

**Downlight**

Luminaire that directs light downward at angles below the horizontal and can be recessed, surface mounted, or suspended

**Efficacy**

The ratio of light output to energy consumption, measured in lumens per watt (not to be confused with efficiency)

**Efficiency**

The amount of light emitted by a fixture divided by that of the lamp source within (expressed as a percentage)

**Electromagnetic spectrum**

The continuum of radiant energy that delineates types according to their wavelengths. Regions within the electromagnetic spectrum include light, heat, UV waves, radio waves, and X-rays.

**Fiber optics**

Thin and flexible glass or plastic fibers that transmit light throughout their length by total internal reflection. (The light is transmitted across the fiber's length by bouncing off its smooth internal surfaces.)

**Filter**

A device for changing the magnitude or spectral composition (color) of an incident light by transmission or reflection

**Floodlight**

A luminaire designed to control and direct light in a broad beam with less precision than a spotlight. Floodlighting illuminates a broad but specific area to a greater illuminance than its surroundings. The terminology is typically applied to outdoor lighting.

**Footcandle (FC)**

The English unit of measurement for illuminance on a surface, described as one lumen per square foot

**Fovea**

The region of the retina responsible for central vision and composed entirely of cones; see retina

**Fluorescent**

A lamp technology consisting of a glass tube lined with phosphors and filled with a low-pressure mercury vapor. An electric arc is passed through the mercury vapor, which emits UV radiation inside the lamp. This excites the phosphors, which in turn emit white light, or fluoresce, from the tube surface. It is characterized by its diffuse white light, along with a relatively high efficacy and long lamp life.

## Glare

The effect of overly bright luminance within the normal field of view, sufficient to cause annoyance, discomfort, or loss of visual performance

## Halogen

Also called a tungsten halogen or quartz lamp, it uses a typical incandescent-tungsten filament in a halogen gas–filled quartz capsule. The lamp operates at a higher temperature, improving the efficiency, output, and life of the incandescent filament. Halogen sources have the advantage of a very high CRI and near-infinite dimming capability.

## Hard light

Also called crisp light, it is a characteristic describing illumination that has crisp-edged or sharply defined shadows.

## High-intensity discharge (HID)

Generic term describing electric discharge technologies that typically utilize short arcs and high wattages. HID technologies include metal halide, mercury vapor, and high-pressure sodium.

## High-pressure sodium

A lamp technology using a short arc in a pressurized capsule filled with sodium and mercury vapor. It is characterized by its very high efficacy but low CRI, as well as its yellow-amber color. High-pressure sodium is considered an HID source.

## Incandescent

A lamp technology that passes a current through a filament, typically tungsten, heating it to the point of emitting light, or incandescence. Incandescent lamps are characterized by their warm, delicate light but short life and inefficiency.

## Illuminance

Term describing the amount of light illuminating a surface. Properly defined as luminous flux (measure of the perceived power of light) incident to a surface measured perpendicular to the illuminated plane per unit area. It is expressed either as lumens per square foot and measured in footcandles, or as lumens per square meter and measured in lux.

## Indirect lighting

Light involving luminaires that direct most of their light toward a room surface, relying on the resulting luminance of that surface to provide or contribute to the functional illuminance of the space

## Infrared radiation (IR)

Describes the region of the electromagnetic spectrum between visible light and radio waves.

Unlike UV, infrared radiation is not generally considered harmful, but can have ramifications due to radiative heat transfer.

## Kelvin

A temperature scale where one unit kelvin is equal to one unit centigrade, but with zero kelvin set to equal an absolute absence of thermal energy corresponding to approximately -273° Celsius. This scale is used to describe the color temperature of a light source.

## Lamp

The technical term for a source designed to emit optical radiation

## Lens

A clear or translucent element in a fixture to control the direction and/or distribution of light passing through it

## Light-emitting diode (LED)

Also referred to as a solid-state diode, this lamp technology consists of a semiconductor that emits light when voltage is applied.

## Light

Radiant energy or electromagnetic radiation that is capable of being perceived visually. Light nominally occurs between 380 nanometers and 780 nanometers in the electromagnetic spectrum. (also called visual radiation)

## Linear source

A lamp or luminaire that can be characterized to emit light along a perceptible length. Linear sources are diffuse in one axis and a point source in the other axis. They are typically described in contrast with a point source or diffuse source.

## Louver

An assembly of baffles or blades to shield glare from normal viewing angles, typically assembled in a geometric array, parallel with the main path of light, and designed to have minimum impact on overall light output

## Low-pressure sodium

A lamp technology using an electric discharge through low-pressure sodium vapor. It is characterized by its very high efficacy but very low CRI.

## Low voltage

A reduced current from the typical main or line voltage. It is used in areas requiring additional protection from wiring or lamps using higher voltages, or for lamp sources requiring a reduced

or highly controlled current. Typical low-voltage sources are halogen or LED, and require a transformer to reduce the voltage for the lamp.

## Lumen

The unit of light flow or luminous flux. One lumen is defined as being equal to the light emitted in a solid angle by a point source having a uniform luminous intensity of one candela. The lumen output is the measure of total light emitted by a source.

## Luminaire

A complete lighting unit or fixture consisting of the lamp source, the lamp holder, any reflector or lenses to control the light, any shielding to control glare, and a connection to a power source. It also includes all accessories and control gear considered part of the final unit.

## Luminance

The amount of light emitted from a surface, describing the brightness of the surface. The units of luminance are footlambert (fL, though this unit is not commonly used) or candelas per square foot or square meter.

## Luminous flux

The visual portion of the flow of radiant flux or energy. Where the total measure of radiant energy is technically the watt, the visual portion is weighted according to our ability to perceive the various portions of the spectrum and is measured in lumens.

## Lux

The metric unit of measurement for illuminance on a surface, described as one lumen per square meter

## Matte

Describes a surface from which the incident light is reflected diffusely, or has that dominant characteristic. It is the opposite of specular.

## Mercury vapor

A lamp technology using an electric discharge through mercury vapor. It is characterized by its blue-green hue and high UV output. It is sometimes used in combination with a phosphor coating for whiter light. The technology is still prevalent in plant-growth facilities and in applications for UV light sources. Mercury vapor is considered an HID source.

## Metal halide

A lamp technology using a short arc in a capsule filled with several rare-earth metal salts, called metal halides, and mercury vapor. It is characterized by its balance of HID efficiency and lamp life with a broad-spectrum white light. Ceramic metal halide is a subgroup, characterized by smaller arc tubes and lower wattages capable of substituting for less-efficient halogen sources. Metal halide is considered an HID source.

### Nanometer (nm)

A metric unit equal to $10^{-9}$ meters, and the common unit for wavelengths of light in the visible spectrum. The wavelengths of light describe the color characteristics of a light.

### Photocell

A light-sensing system component that controls luminaires and dimmers in response to detected light levels

### Photometry

The measurement of quantities associated with light. Photometric reports generated from laboratory testing or computer simulations typically describe the geometric distribution and efficacy of a lamp source or efficiency of a luminaire.

### Photopic vision

Vision mediated entirely by the cones on the retina. Associated with high-level luminance, photopic vision is capable of discerning colors due to the three types of cone receptors associated with the three primary colors.

### Point source

A lamp or luminaire that can be characterized to emit light from a point. Point source light will tend to have crisp shadows and is perceived as more dramatic. It is typically described in contrast with a linear source or diffuse source.

### Projector

A luminaire designed to produce a very precise and narrow beam of even intensity, usually using a combination of either a parabolic or ellipsoidal reflector and lenses. It is typically used for precise spotlighting, framing objects, or projecting images through a pattern lens.

### Rated lamp life

The mean value of estimated life or usable life, determined by a lamp manufacturer from laboratory testing

### Recessed

A term used to describe a light fixture fully recessed into an architectural condition, with the light aperture nearly flush with the surface

### Reflector

The portion of a lamp or luminaire designed to direct or control the light distribution of the light bouncing off of it

### Retina

A light-sensitive membrane lining the posterior inner surface of the eye, composed of rods and cones. Rods are retinal receptors that respond to low levels of luminance and are sensitive to shorter wavelengths near the UV spectrum, while cones are retinal receptors that dominate the retinal response when the luminance level is high, with three types responding to a range of wavelengths that we associate with primary colors: red, green, and blue. The combined sensitivity of all three types of cones provides the basis for the perception of color. The central region of the retina, the fovea, is responsible for the most distinct vision and is composed entirely of cones.

### Scotopic vision

Vision mediated entirely by the rods on the retina. Associated with low-level luminance, scotopic vision is not capable of discerning colors properly due to its single visual receptor, and is also incapable of discerning fine detail due to the lack of rods in the fovea or central region of the eye and due to their sparsity compared with the cones. Also see photopic vision.

### Soft light

A characteristic describing illumination that has soft-edged or poorly defined shadows

### Spectral power distribution (SPD)

A visual profile of the color characteristics of a given light source. An SPD represents the radiant power of a source emitted per wavelength or range of wavelengths in the visible portion of the electromagnetic spectrum.

### Specular

Describes a surface that reflects light such that the angle of reflection is equal to that of incidence. It is the opposite of matte.

### Task lighting

Lighting that is directed to a specific surface to provide illumination for visual tasks

### Translucent

A characteristic of a material or surface describing the partial or diffuse transmission of light

### Transparent

A characteristic of a material or surface describing the transmission of light without significant diffusion, such that images behind the material can be seen distinctly

### Ultraviolet (UV) radiation

Describes the region of the electromagnetic spectrum between x-rays and visible light. For practical purposes, this is the spectrum from 100 nanometers to 400 nanometers.

### Uplight

Luminaire that directs light upward at angles above the horizontal

### Vision

The ability to perceive the luminance of surfaces by the radiant energy entering the eye and stimulating the retina

### Voltage

The electric potential difference between two points in a circuit, equal to wattage divided by amperage. The standard unit of measurement for electric potential and electromotive force is the volt.

### Wallwasher

Describes a luminaire designed to smoothly illuminate a vertical surface

### Wattage

The electric power or electric flux of a light source, equal to voltage times amperage. It describes the rate of energy consumption of a luminaire when in use. The standard unit of measurement for all energy flux including electric is the watt. See luminous flux.

### Wavelength

A characteristic of radiant flux that describes where it occurs on the electromagnetic spectrum. Typically, radiant flux is composed of electromagnetic radiation in a range of wavelengths. Technically, wavelength is the distance between two successive points on a periodic wave in the direction of propagation where the oscillation has the same phase. The unit of measurement for wavelengths of radiant flux in the visual spectrum is the nanometer.

# Bibliography

Alekan, Henri. *Des Lumieres et des Ombres*. Paris: Librairie du Collectionneur, 1991.

Barzel, Amnon. *Light Art: Targetti Light Art Collection*. Milan: Skira, 2006.

Brandston, Howard. *Learning to See: A Matter of Light*. New York: Illuminating Engineering Society of North America, 2008.

Büttiker, Urs. *Louis I. Kahn: Light and Space*. Basel, Switzerland: Birkhäuser Verlag, 1993.

Clark, B. A. J. "Outdoor Lighting and Crime, Part 1: Little or no Benefit." Victoria: Astronomical Society of Victoria, 2003. http://amper.ped.muni.cz/light/crime/lp040_1h.html.

———. "Outdoor Lighting and Crime, Part 2: Coupled Growth." Victoria: Astronomical Society of Victoria, 2003. http://amper.ped.muni.cz/light/crime/OLCpt2.htm.

Davidson, Marshall B. "Early American Lighting." *The Metropolitan Museum of Art Bulletin*, New Series 3, no. 1 (Summer 1944): 30–40.

Descottes, Hervé. *Ultimate Lighting Design: Projects by Hervé Descottes / L'Observatoire International*. New York: teNeues, 2005.

Egan, M. David, and Victor W. Olgyay. *Architectural Lighting*, 2nd ed. Boston: McGraw-Hill, 2002.

Eliasson, Olafur. *Your Engagement has Consequences on the Relativity of Your Reality*. Baden, Switzerland: Lars Müller Publishers, 2006.

Futagawa, Yukio, ed. *Light & Space: Modern Architecture*. Tokyo: ADA EDITA, 1994.

Goethe, Johann Wolfgang von. *Theory of Colours*. Translated by Charles L. Eastlake. Cambridge, MA: MIT Press, 1970.

Gordon, Gary. *Interior Lighting for Designers*, 4th ed. Hoboken, NJ: John Wiley & Sons, 2003.

Haas, O. F. "Planning the Street Lighting System." *Planning for City Traffic: Annals of the American Academy of Political and Social Science* 133 (Sept. 1927): 34–49.

Hays, K. Michael, ed. *Architecture Theory Since 1968*. Cambridge, MA: MIT Press, 2000.

Henle, Mary, ed. *Vision and Artifact*. New York: Springer Publishing Co., 1976.

Hyman, Isabelle, and Marvin Trachtenberg. *Architecture: From Prehistory to Post-modernism*. New York: Harry N. Abrams, Inc., 1986.

International Dark Sky Association. "Light Pollution and Safety." 2008. http://docs.darksky.org/Docs/ida_safety_brochure.pdf.

Narboni, Roger. *La Lumiere Urbaine: Eclairer les Espaces Publics*. Paris: Le Moniteur, 1995.

Le Corbusier. *Ronchamp*. Stuttgart, Germany: Verlag Gerd Hatje, 1957.

Lennox Moyer, Janet. *The Landscape Lighting Book*, 2nd ed. Hoboken, NJ: John Wiley & Sons, 2005.

Livingstone, Margaret. *Vision and Art: The Biology of Seeing*. New York: Harry N. Abrams, Inc., 2002.

Lowther, Clare, and Sarah Schultz, eds. *Bright: Architectural Illumination and Light Installations*. Amsterdam: Frame Publishers, 2008.

Millet, Marietta S. *Light Revealing Architecture*. New York: Van Nostrand Reinhold, 1996.

Narboni, Roger. *Lighting the Landscape: Art Design Technologies*. Basel, Switzerland: Birkhäuser, 2004.

Neumann, Dietrich. *Architecture of the Night: The Illuminated Building*. New York: Prestel, 2002.

Noever, Peter, ed. *James Turrell: The Other Horizon*. Ostfildern-Ruit, Germany: Hatje Cantz Verlag, 1999.

Plummer, Henry. *Masters of Light, First Volume: Twentieth-century Pioneers*. Tokyo: A+U, 2003.

———. *The Architecture of Natural Light*. New York: The Monacelli Press, 2009.

Rasmussen, Steen Eiler. *Experiencing Architecture*. Cambridge, MA: MIT Press, 1986.

Rea, Mark S., ed. *The IESNA Lighting Handbook: Reference & Application*, 9th ed. New York: Illuminating Engineering Society of North America, 2000.

Schivelbusch, Wolfgang. *Disenchanted Night: The Industrialization of Light in the Nineteenth Century*. Berkeley: The University of California Press, 1988.

Steffy, Gary R. *Architectural Lighting Design*. Hoboken, NJ: John Wiley & Sons, 2008.

Tanizaki, Jun'ichirō. *In Praise of Shadows*. New Haven, CT: Leete's Island Books, 1977.

Pradel, Jean-Louis. *Yann Kersalé: Lumiere Matiere*. France: Editions BäS, 1990.

Turrell, James. *Occluded Front: James Turrell*. Edited by Julia Brown. Los Angeles: Fellows of Contemporary Art and the Lapis Press, 1985.

———. *Eclipse: James Turrell*. Ostfildern-Ruit, Germany: Hatje Cantz Verlag, 1999.

Weibel, Peter, and Gregor Jansen, eds. *Light Art from Artificial Light: Light as a Medium in 20th and 21st Century Art*. Ostfildern-Ruit, Germany: Hatje Cantz Verlag, 2006.

## Image Credits

Figure F.1: © Rene Burri, courtesy Magnum Photos

Figures 1.1–1.3, 1.8–1.10, 1.12, 2.1–2.5, 2.8, 2.10, 2.12, 3.1, 3.3–3.9, 3.13–3.15, 3.18, 4.1, 4.3, 4.6–4.8, 5.2, 5.5, 5.9, 5.10, 5.11, 6.1, 6.2a–6.2f, 7.2, 7.5, 7.6, 7.9, 8.2, 9.2, 10.2, 11.2. 11.3, 11.6, 12.2, 12.3: Anna Muzlimova

Figures 1.4, 6.3a, 6.3b, 7.1, 8.1, 9.1, 10.1, 11.1, 12.1: Cecilia E. Ramos

Figure 1.5: © Lars Frick

Figure 1.6: © James Turrell, photo by Florian Holzherr, courtesy the Mattress Factory

Figures 1.7a and 1.7b: © Todd Carlson

Figures 1.11a–1.11d: © L'Observatoire International

Figure 1.13 and all appendix graphics from pp. 134–38: Socorro Sperati

Figure 2.6: © Geoff DeOld

Figure 2.7: © Julie M. Peng

Figures 2.9, 11.4, 11.9: © Paul Warchol

Figures 2.11, 10.4–10.6: © Yusheng Liao

Figures 2.13a and 2.13b: © George Fleenor

Figures 2.14, 4.9, 6.7: B. Alex Miller

Figure 2.15: Georges de la Tour, *The Education of the Virgin* (1650, oil on canvas) 33 in. x 39 1/2 in. (83.82 cm x 100.33 cm). Purchased by the Frick Collection, 1948 © The Frick Collection, New York

Figure 2.16: courtesy Toyo Ito and Yamagiwa.

Figure 2.17: Léon Gimpel, *Paris, Salon d'Automne* (1903). Plaque de projection, 9 x12 cm © Coll. Société française de photographie

Figures 2.18, 3.17, 4.4, 4.5, 8.6, 11.5, 11.7, 11.10, 12.6, 12.8, 12.10: © Hervé Descottes

Figures 3.2a–3.2f: courtesy of General Electric Company

Figure 3.10: Claude Monet, French, 1840–1926, *Stacks of Wheat (Sunset, Snow Effect)* (1890/91), oil on canvas 25 11/16 in. x 39 1/2 in. (65.3 cm x 100.4 cm), Potter Palmer Collection, 1922.431, the Art Institute of Chicago (photography © The Art Institute of Chicago) © The Art Institute of Chicago

Figure 3.11: Georges Seurat (1859–91), study for *A Sunday on La Grande Jatte* (1884–85), oil on canvas, 27 3/4 in. x 41 in. (70.5 cm x 104.1 cm), bequest of Sam A. Lewisohn, 1951 (51.112.6), the Metropolitan Museum of Art, New York, NY, U.S.A. (© The Metropolitan Museum of Art / Art Resource, NY) © The Metropolitan Museum of Art / Art Resource, NY

Figure 3.12: photograph © Christian Beirle González, © 2010 Stephen Flavin / Artist Rights Society (ARS), New York

Figure 3.16: © Jean-Pierre Duplan, courtesy Agence Patrick Jouin

Figure 3.19: © Simon Watson, courtesy Hotels AB

Figure 4.2: © George Steinmetz

Figure 5.1: Robert Irwin, *Light and Space* (2007), 115 fluorescent lights one wall 271 1/4 x 620 in., Collection Museum of Contemporary Art San Diego, Museum purchase with funds from the Annenberg Foundation © 2010 Robert Irwin / Artist Rights Society (ARS), New York; photo by Philipp Scholz Rittermann courtesy Museum of Contemporary Art San Diego

Figure 5.3: © Horst Kiechle

Figure 5.4: © NASA/NOAA/DMSP

Figure 5.6: © Xavier Rotivel

Figure 5.7: © NASA/JPL/GLIMPSE

Figure 5.8: © Ricky Ridecós

Figure 6.4a–6.4f: © Cecilia E. Ramos, sculpture by J. Cheh courtesy Liz Belomlinsky

Figures 6.5, 6.6a–6.6c: © Ruth Waltz, courtesy Byrd Hoffman Watermill Foundation and Robert Wilson Archive

Figure 6.8: © Gabriele Pranzo-Zaccaria

Figure 6.9: courtesy Bibliothèque Nationale de France

Figures 7.3, 7.4, 7.7, 7.8, 8.4, 8.5, 9.3–9.6: © Eric Laignel

Figure 7.10: © 2009 Emile Dubuisson

Figures 8.3, 8.8: © 2008 Walter Dufresne, Photographer, walterdufresne.com

Figure 8.7: © Amer Maleh

Figure 10.3 © Lyu Hanabusa

Figure 11.8: © Timo Kiukkola

Figures 12.4, 12.5, 12.9: © Roland Halbe

Figure 12.7: © Peiheng Tsai

Figures 13.1, 13.5, 13.6: © Andy Ryan

Figures 13.2–13.4: courtesy Steven Holl

Figure 14.1: *Plafonnier à plumes*, 1998, brass, oak, duck feathers, 17.4 cm x 21.5 cm x 30 cm © Eric Morin, courtesy Sylvain Dubuisson

Figure 15.1: Albert Bierstadt, *Sierra Nevada Morning*, 1870, from the collection of Gilcrease Museum, Tulsa, Oklahoma.

Figure 15.2: © Mike Falco

Figure 15.3: © Iwan Baan

Figure 16.9: © Thomas Mayer

Endpage images: © 2010 Stephen Flavin / Artist Rights Society (ARS), New York; photos © Vanessa Thaureau

The light goes off through a path of reflections

and comes back to itself:

a hand that invents itself, an eye

that sees itself in its own inventions.


Light is time thinking about itself.


—Octavio Paz, "Sight and Touch (for Balthus)"